Quality in Distance Education

Focus on On-Line Learning

Katrina A. Meyer

ASHE-ERIC Higher Education Report: Volume 29, Number 4
Adrianna J. Kezar, Series Editor

Prepared and published by

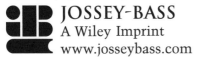 **JOSSEY-BASS**
A Wiley Imprint
www.josseybass.com

In cooperation with

ERIC Clearinghouse on Higher Education
The George Washington University
URL: www.eriche.org

Association for the Study
of Higher Education
URL: www.tiger.coe.missouri.edu/~ashe

Graduate School of Education and Human Development
The George Washington University
URL: www.gwu.edu

#51273280

Quality in Distance Education: Focus on On-Line Learning
Katrina A. Meyer
ASHE-ERIC Higher Education Report: Volume 29, Number 4
Adrianna J. Kezar, Series Editor

This publication was prepared partially with funding from the Office of
Educational Research and Improvement, U.S. Department of Education, under
contract no. ED-99-00-0036. The opinions expressed in this report do not
necessarily reflect the positions or policies of OERI or the Department.

ISSN 0884-0040   electronic ISSN 1536-0709   ISBN 0-7879-6349-6

The ASHE-ERIC Higher Education Report is part of the Jossey-Bass Higher
and Adult Education Series and is published six times a year by Wiley Subscription
Services, Inc., A Wiley Company, at Jossey-Bass, 989 Market Street, San Francisco,
California 94103-1741.

For subscription information, see the Back Issue/Subscription Order Form
in the back of this journal.

CALL FOR PROPOSALS: Prospective authors are strongly encouraged to contact
Adrianna Kezar at (301) 405-0868 or kezar@wam.umd.edu.

Visit the Jossey-Bass Web site at **www.josseybass.com.**

Printed in the United States of America on acid-free recycled paper.

Executive Summary

Writings about Web-based learning are fraught with misunderstandings, misperceptions, and mistakes. Undertaking this project has been an eye-opener for me, and reading this report will likely be a surprise to the reader as well. The main questions below express most of these misperceptions—and hard-earned insights.

Does the Research Reviewed Apply Only to Distance Education?

This monograph focuses on the research concerning on-line learning, and although it makes some mention of other modes of distance education, it is oriented toward exploring the specific intricacies of learning over the Web. *Distance education* is a broader term, comprising several different delivery modes. *On-line* or *Web-based* distance education is use of the Web to deliver education whether at a distance or next door, although the Web may also be used to enhance on-campus courses in particular ways. Most of the research reviewed may actually be quite interesting and useful to faculty incorporating the Web in their regular classes. And because the line between Web-based learning at a distance and in an on-campus course is murky at best, research on campus-based uses of the Web is also included in the review.

Focusing on on-line education should not be construed as an attempt to ignore some of the fine work of early distance education theorists and researchers. In many cases, this work holds up quite well and can be constructively applied to on-line learning. Many good reviews of this earlier research exist (Gibson, 1990; Moore and Thompson, 1997), but they are beyond the purview of the current monograph, which focuses on on-line learning.

But There Isn't Much Research on Using the Web, Is There?

I had been operating under two misconceptions, which have been duly erased. I thought there would not be much research on on-line learning: I was not only wrong but gravely wrong. I found numerous papers (not included in this review, as they do not describe a research study) where faculty discussed their personal experiences with on-line learning and generated thoughtful and useful insights into how best to use the medium. Literally hundreds of studies had been peer reviewed and published in on-line journals or posted on conference Web sites. Many faculty in Canada, Australia, England, and the United States have been busy conducting their own research into on-line learning, using some very innovative approaches or more classic experimental designs.

I also thought I would need to rely on the research literature in other domains (e.g., cognitive science) but had to do so less than expected. I was also wrong in thinking that the research might still be focused on such outcomes as student achievement without looking at the intervening variables (in the student, the environment, even the instructional design) that might explain the outcome. I saw some of these types of studies, although we need more.

But Aren't These Studies Poorly Done?

The perception is that most studies done on distance education or the use of technology are poorly designed and prone to incomplete analyses. That certainly is true of the simple comparison study, where student outcomes (such as course grades) for an on-line course are compared with a traditional course. It is the source of the "no significant differences" phenomenon, where possible intervening forces are ignored and the researcher and instructor are the same person, further muddying the results. No one would argue that this design is flawed and the results questionable. And I would be happy if I never saw another such study published anywhere.

Some very good studies are out there, however—some of them quantitative and others qualitative and still others a thoughtful or theoretical analysis of what is going on in an on-line course. Some of these studies are quite creative and use interesting approaches to analyze the on-line course or the student learning resulting from using the Web in a course, e.g., applying critical analyses to student understanding implied in his or her contributions to threaded discussions. Many of these studies would pass the harshest peer review criteria, and others are less complicated but no less worth reading. Even though we may value multivariate, controlled-environment research, it is sometimes the serious and balanced personal voice of the writer sharing his or her insights that may influence other faculty members to try the new medium or improve their use of it as an instructional tool.

Will We Ever Have a Definitive Answer on the Quality of On-Line Learning?

It is unlikely we will ever unravel all the factors that impact on-line learning. It is complex and its elements (the technology and the students) keep changing. Because we have not achieved a definitive answer on quality for more traditional classroom situations, perhaps it is unwise to expect such clarity for on-line learning. But more understanding is always better than less, so the search for clarity will (and should) continue.

I remain a supporter of on-line learning and think it holds great promise for students who wish or need to learn this way. It forces faculty and institutions to question assumptions and renew their attention to student learning. No student of technology can pretend that any technology is always and unfailingly positive, however, and I urge others to undertake some of the longitudinal and careful studies of this learning to see whether the Web may have some secondary or tertiary impacts—the unintended consequences technology is famous for—that we cannot see at the present. Most technologies are likely to have such impacts, so it is wise to keep a careful eye on what they might be. In the meantime, however, having doubts about technology is no reason for keeping it away from students, for they may be better able to identify what the problems may be and excuse themselves when they feel it is right to do so.

What Might Be the Most Important Lesson to Take from This Review?

Probably because so much of the earlier research on distance education was the simple comparison study, results were attributed to the use of technology without any attention to the instructional design of the course or the instructional uses of a most flexible tool, the Web. If there is one lesson I would most like to pound home, it is that one cannot evaluate the use of technology separately from the instructional uses made of it. Smith and Dillon (1999) call it the *media/method confound,* and it is perhaps as clear a term for the interrelationship between technology and instructional design as I have found. In other words, it is not the technology that has an effect, it is the way it is used.

If I could have a second most important lesson, it would be based on the work of Reeves and Nass (1996), who studied the relationship between media and reality. They found that people treat media as though it were real life, which can be attributed to the need and expectation for human relationships, even if you are relating only to a computer. Basic human psychology is the key to unlocking our relationship with the Web, and perhaps it explains why instructional design is so important and why we can create community over a bunch of wires.

And if I could be indulged for a third most important lesson, it would be to urge caution when reading so many opinion pieces on Web-based distance education. As may soon become clear, the researcher's biases can wend their way into the research design and the interpretation of the results, leaving the reader wondering about the true worth of the study. Be a critical reader; although there is nothing wrong with advocacy, beware of advocacy disguised as research.

So How Would You Define Quality?

Although Chapter Five gives several examples of measures for quality Web-based learning, I would recommend focusing predominantly on student learning and augment it with those variables that contribute to learning. Quality learning is largely the result of ample interaction with the faculty, other students, and content. Because the Web enables interaction, it provides an opportunity for faculty to construct collaborative projects for students. A quality course or program would allow for multiple paths to learning, capitalizing on students' different learning styles or intelligences. Quality would also be the result of opportunities for students to construct meaning from experiences, to reflect on meaning, and to test and retest those understandings in new situations. These definitions are not too dissimilar from those of a quality education, so the only difference is that on-line learning uses the Web to make these opportunities available to students in class or at a distance.

And if you do not have the time and resources, focus exclusively on student learning. Student learning is the ultimate reason why higher education exists, and so we need to know how to define, assess, and improve student learning in multiple ways.

Where Is Research Needed?

As long as you do not undertake a comparison study, there is plenty to do and many answers to seek. If I could promote one of the areas that is most needed, it is finding an answer (or answers) to the question of which technology works with which student and which learning objective in which discipline and why. Let me add a plea for answers to the question about what mix of media (including, of course, face-to-face instruction) works best for which purpose. And because we always need to keep a close eye on the legitimate worries of the technology critics, we must ask whether any evidence exists that the Web is having any deleterious effects or unintended consequences on students or their learning. Undoubtedly, the careful reader will find many more areas for research in this document, and I hope they do so and do so quickly.

Are There Some Unforeseen Benefits to Doing Research on the Web?

The Web also drastically changed how I conducted this review. I am grateful that so many of the conferences focused on using the Web for teaching in higher education have made it a practice to make individual papers available on-line, and I am grateful as well that so many peer-reviewed journals put their contents on-line. This availability made searching for studies somewhat easier, and it means that you will also find these papers at the Web sites indicated in the reference list. Although several fine journals still publish in print, finding good peer-reviewed papers on-line is both quicker and easier for those of us interested in learning from others' experiences and for the researcher interested in sharing his or her results.

What About the Connection Between Quality and Cost?

If I have one regret, it is that I could not spend too much time on the quality/cost nexus: the interconnections between raising quality and lowering cost (or improving efficiency). In light of the large number of good studies on quality alone, I chose to focus on those elements that most contribute to quality learning. Van Dusen (2000) provides a good discussion of the interrelationship of cost and quality, and a growing number of studies look at cost and quality, most particularly Twigg's Center for Academic Transformation and the studies on asynchronous learning networks funded by the Sloan Foundation. Obviously, more needs to be done on this topic, but these sources are excellent places to begin a review of the research on whether one can improve quality *and* efficiency at the same time.

Is This Report the Definitive Answer?

No. Given how rapidly faculty are producing research on Web-based education and how our use of the Web changes from year to year, this document may be out of date in a few years, when another review of the research should be undertaken. Or in other words, as researchers continue their study of online learning, the results of research included in this review may be superseded by new and better understandings of what works best and why. That is a humbling truth, but at least it ensures that we must stay current or lose our place in the rapid advance of the field. Although using the Web in education is sometimes fraught with problems—downed servers, inadequate ISPs, bug-prone software, and even viruses that are communicated by e-mail—any errors or inadequacies found in this document have an all-too-human source.

Contents

Foreword

No topic has received so much attention in the last decade as technology, and possibly no topic is as misunderstood or has received as little attention as distance education. Correspondence and other forms of distance education have been mostly ignored in the higher education research literature. The connection of technology with distance education has opened the door among researchers who typically ignored this large sector of higher education. Issues that are outside the core of institutional practices are often subordinated. In fact, as the author notes, people see distance education not only as subordinate but also at some level a threat to traditional practices of teaching and learning. Therefore, the few articles or books that are written tend to come from a mostly negative ideological orientation. But there appear to be policymakers and administrators who see that distance education is becoming more closely aligned with the core of institutional practice and realize we need unbiased research and information to guide decision making about this misunderstood area of institutional operation. This monograph is revolutionary in its attempts to bring distance education to the forefront of educational dialogues, especially in its basis on research.

Katrina Meyer has spent many years working in policymaking and research related to distance education, and she brings this experience to the development of an authoritative monograph. She is currently an assistant professor of educational leadership at the University of North Dakota, with a special interest in Web-based learning and distance education in higher education institutions. For more than thirteen years, she has worked in administration and policy at the state and institutional levels in distance learning and technology.

Meyer's willingness to engage in the messy debates about what counts as research, dilemmas in methodology, and contradictory or nonsignificant findings is most impressive. She also takes on the elusive questions related to quality. Perhaps no other topic is so important to higher education but so illusory. Most scholars skirt quality questions and focus on descriptive reports of trends among institutions involved in distance education and other easy, less complex questions. To directly engage quality in distance education and the contradictory findings of research is confusing, convoluted, and fraught with peril—at best! Moreover, new research is conducted regularly, and the topic is a moving target. Meyer's goal is to provide a contingent framework for making decisions based on existing research and normative guidelines. This same framework can be built on for future decision making as new research emerges. Countries worldwide are also seeking to understand and make sense of the confusing research on quality; this monograph should prove useful for these many international discussions as well.

Several ASHE-ERIC monographs focus on related topics. Gerald Van Dusen has written two monographs on issues related to technology and distance education. His most recent monograph, *The Digital Dilemma,* focuses on the problems of access that policymakers and educational leaders need to consider when exploring distance education. His earlier monograph, *The Virtual Campus,* examines the administrative processes, institutional facilitators, and barriers of integrating technology in the classroom. Jeffrey Cantor's *Higher Education Outside the Academy* is a helpful resource on distance education in corporate training and in the for-profit sectors. Trends in this arena are extremely helpful for traditional higher education to observe and learn from, as they are often more advanced in the use of these newer forms of technology. Armed with these resources, educational leaders will have a wealth of information on the most vexing issues—quality, access, implementation—related to distance education.

Adrianna J. Kezar
Series Editor

The Explosion of
Distance Education

THE ENORMOUS AND RAPID GROWTH of distance education and enrollments in Web-based courses has generated interest in defining quality for on-line learning. Whether on-line learning becomes the norm in higher education or remains an auxiliary to existing approaches is a matter that only time will resolve. In the meantime, a number of groups are deeply interested in understanding how to ensure that course work or degree programs using this technology are of high quality. Whether it is the federal government or state governments, accrediting associations or students, all stress the need to have a better understanding of what contributes to quality in on-line learning.

Whether it is the federal government or state governments, accrediting associations or students, all stress the need to have a better understanding of what contributes to quality in on-line learning.

Recent Growth of Distance Education

Although to many, distance education may seem a new phenomenon, various earlier forms have existed for decades. Correspondence study began in the late 1800s and has been a part of many institutions since the early 1900s (Moore, 1990), as has the tradition of faculty traveling to off-campus locations to meet with local students. To alleviate the requirement for travel (by either the faculty or students), institutions have used audio connections (e.g., telephone), videotapes, and television. From the early 1980s on, satellite telecommunications were used to transmit largely one-way broadcasting to off-campus locations, although later uses of satellite allowed for two-way audio communications via telephone connections. This use was rapidly followed by microwave-based interactive video from the late 1980s onward and then, increasingly throughout the 1990s, installation of land-based systems for interactive video. Interactive or compressed video allowed one-way (teacher to student) visual connection (usually through microwave links) and then two-way communications providing both visual and audio connections. Whether the network was microwave or fiber connections, it enhanced access to distance education classes that more nearly mirrored the current practices of on-campus classrooms, including visual and audio communications, two-way conversations between and among faculty and students. Chapter Two reviews some of the research on the effectiveness of these forms of distance education, but suffice it for now to remark that interactive video—although an improvement over more traditional forms of distance education—was still tied to occurring in one place (duly equipped with appropriate connections and transmitting/receiving equipment) and at one set time.

With the advent of first the Internet and then the Web, however, came a growing comprehension that education need not be site- or time-bound. And although this comprehension was slow in developing (as was the networking and software to support such a vision), once the potential was grasped, the boom was on.

For instance, the National Center for Education Statistics (1999b) found that from fall 1995 to academic year 1997–98, the percentage of higher education institutions offering distance education increased from 33 percent to 44 percent. Public institutions, however, were more likely to be involved in distance education, with 72 percent of two-year and 79 percent of four-year institutions offering courses. In the same time frame, the number of courses and degree or certificate programs doubled, from 25,730 to 52,270 courses and from 860 to 1,520 programs. Student enrollments also doubled, from 753,640 to 1.6 million. And although institutions' use of interactive video stayed approximately steady at 56 percent during this period of time, use of the Internet grew to 60 percent of institutions in 1997–98.

This doubling of effort (courses and programs) and student response from 1995 to 1997–98 is a tribute to institutional entrepreneurialism, even though at times the demand for and potential seen for Web-based distance education outpaced what higher education could currently provide. This situation was largely because of the parallel boom in Internet use in other areas: business, K–12 education, and personal use in the home.

The Digital Explosion

Readers should remember that any data reported here will likely be out of date soon, especially as growth outstrips publication schedules. With this proviso in mind, many existing and new businesses have begun to provide Web-based services to consumers; of the fifty-four jobs expected to grow significantly by 2005, only eight do not require technological fluency (U.S. Department of Labor, 2001). In K–12 education in 1999, 63 percent of classrooms were connected to the Internet, and 95 percent of the nation's schools had such connections (National Center for Education Statistics, 1999a). From one-third (National Telecommunications Information Agency, 1999) to one-half (Dataquest, 1999) of homes have Internet access, although this distribution is weighted heavily in favor of families with higher incomes, who are white, younger, and living in urban settings (National Telecommunications Information Agency, 1999; Lenhart, 2000). Data from UCLA's Internet report (2001) found that 72.3 percent of Americans go on-line, they are most satisfied with the Internet's ability to help them communicate with other people, almost half (48.9 percent) made purchases on-line, and Internet users tend to spend more time with friends and family, with the big loser being watching television. Not surprisingly then, students who arrive in postsecondary settings are more likely to have and be able to use a computer, send e-mail, and browse the Web. A recent study (Hanson and Jubeck, 1999) is illustrative: of 280 college students responding to the survey, 71 percent had a computer, 73 percent had Internet access, 93 percent had sent an e-mail, and 100 percent had browsed the Web.

The always interesting annual survey called *The Campus Computing Project* (http://www.campuscomputing.net) provides information on how higher education campuses are meeting the challenges of information technology. For several early years in the 1990s, the biggest challenge was installing networks and computer stations and then ensuring they were maintained and upgraded regularly. Then institutions began to develop on-line services, such as putting campus information or a course catalog on a Web site. Then there was the challenge of helping faculty integrate technology into teaching and expanding services to students. In the latest survey, Green (2001) found 87 percent of campuses provide college applications on-line, 55 percent provide course registration over the Web, and 56 percent offer some fully on-line courses. The latest challenges include eCommerce services (e.g., use of credit cards to pay tuition on-line) and coping with budget cuts in academic computing. But "helping faculty integrate technology into instruction" has been the single "most important IT [information technology] issue" for several years (and will likely continue to be for several more). There is good news as well: 73.2 percent of institutions in the survey have established a single course management software package to help faculty design courses with standard configurations for all students at the institution, and 71.5 percent of students own a computer. These figures capture the challenges higher education faces as it meets the new digital future and adjusts to a new student clientele with new demands for services.

Political Initiatives

States have come to support distance education as a way to expand access to rural residents and working adults, because neither population had been well served by higher education. Actions by legislatures and governors have been particularly supportive of distance education, for their own reasons.

The National Education Association (1997) interviewed key legislators and found many that supported use of distance education to expand access, improve student learning, control costs, and improve productivity of faculty and administrative efficiency. Legislatures have also been motivated to encourage the adoption of distance education in efforts to lower costs or costs per unit in higher education (National Education Association, 1997). Legislatures responded to this rosy projection of technology's potential by appropriating more than $370 million in 1996–97 (Mingle, 1998) for higher education technology. Legislators' preconceptions of education as little more than information transfer and acquisition of job skills, however, affect their definition of quality distance education.

The National Governors Association has produced several reports focusing on how governors can reap the benefits of technology, among them *Transforming Learning Through Technology* (1999) on technology in K–12 schools, *The State of E-Learning in the States* (2001a) on postsecondary uses of technology, and *A Vision of E-Learning for America's Workforce* (2001b). The Western Governors University was one such effort aimed at sharing courses and programs across the participating states (and avoiding the cost of developing duplicate courses) and stimulating the adoption of new technologies among higher education institutions in the participating states.

In addition, the U.S. Department of Education's Agenda Project (2001) sought direction on improvements in the Higher Education Act. Distance education was given some prominence, and the department's role in supporting change (and seeking ways to prevent abuse) was emphasized. Although the federal government's role is more constrained than state roles in supporting the growth of distance education, the support of the federal government has been essential in the effort to revise current regulations to remove barriers to new forms of distance education and to extend federal benefits (i.e., student aid) to distance education students.

The Changing Marketplace

Distance education has benefited from and contributed to a growing understanding that the marketplace in which higher education operates is changing. In many states (but certainly not all), its traditional market—i.e., graduating high school seniors—is growing as a result of the baby boom echo working its way through K–12 education. With the advent of technology in the workplace, the number of adults who need continuous professional development and workers who need retraining or new careers is growing. Moreover, technology has enabled people living in communities away from the main campus to consider enrolling in college. The Knight Higher Education

Collaborative (2000) calls this phenomenon a "fundamental broadening and reshaping of the market for learning" (p. 3).

Not surprisingly, the market has responded with the entry of more distance education providers, including public and private higher education institutions, for-profit providers, institutions from overseas such as the British Open University (Palattella, 1998), publishers, and brand new corporations created by multimillion dollar investments to take advantage of the market. (More recently, the collapse of the dot com industry has seen a number of these new entries fail or be absorbed by other competitors.) A consistent criticism of one new provider, the University of Phoenix, was based on a charge of a lack of quality, a charge based on the university's different formats for students. If the university's continued growth in student enrollments is telling, however, perhaps students have voted with their feet, making the University of Phoenix the largest for-profit institution in the United States.

The marketplace has also stimulated new products. Although many offerings are associate's, bachelor's, and master's degrees, competency-based programs are also growing, especially in the IT professional fields. In addition, shorter programs are available, from modules available on-line for just-in-time training to certificate programs in numerous fields of study.

Institutions have responded to the new marketplace in various ways. Some have been drawn into distance education with the goal of serving more students, which results in increased funding in some states (where higher education funding is tied to the number of full-time equivalent students enrolled). Other institutions have pursued the portions of the marketplace where they can create some profits (where there are large numbers of students, or courses are low in cost to design or deliver) to offset stagnant or declining budgets. Data collected by Primary Research Group (1999) found that 87 percent of distance learning programs operate at a profit, which is mirrored by a surge in profits from continuing education programs (Gose, 1999). Although many factors impact whether distance learning can be profitable, it is clear that even more traditional higher education institutions consider themselves players in the new marketplace and that the doubling of enrollments supports the view that they have been successful, at least initially.

Katz and Associates (1999) have discussed at length the "new competition" in higher education as well as its effects on institutions. Although understanding the dynamics of the new competitive marketplace is interesting, it is its impact on quality and perceptions of the importance of quality that are pertinent.

Those who contemplate the forces of the new marketplace have proposed several changes that may occur. For example, the growth of new types of possible students who do not value degrees might result in a lower emphasis on gaining a degree and greater emphasis on gaining competencies, a change that is mirrored by some employers who prefer new hires with proven competencies. With the growth of new types of providers (e.g., publishers), traditional higher education institutions may lose their control over the granting of degrees, and accrediting associations may lose their role as a guarantor of quality. With a greater chase for students and new markets, some hypothesize that quality will decline, while others credit heightened competition for increasing quality. Some presuppose that students do not care for quality, only ease, and others propose that students will always care about quality if their future success is at stake. For higher education, the new marketplace may well create the conditions for a different conception of quality, one more in line with students' needs. It is important to note that no one yet has documented whether these changes are occurring, and thus these statements are guesses of what may occur. And so far, there is no evidence that the new competition has diminished quality, only that quality may have taken on new definitions.

With the growing emphasis on distance education, faculty (e.g., David Noble) have attacked distance education as a suborning of traditional institutional values as institutions pursue profit initiatives. Some have called this the *commodification* of higher education, a charge that is often poorly defined. Legislators talk longingly of the faculty-less course, which is just as poorly conceived, or improving efficiency or productivity. As the marketplace changes and becomes less secure and understood, the focus on the quality of distance education has become an emotional and political issue, with opponents arguing that the new use of technology is, by definition, of poor quality and proponents arguing that on-line course work can produce valuable student learning.

This review focuses strictly on the evidence and arguments surrounding quality rather than issues surrounding reducing costs or improving efficiency. Undoubtedly, a relationship of some kind exists between cost and quality, but a lot more research must to be done to flesh out these relationships. In the meantime, many researchers are focusing on understanding and improving the quality of on-line learning, and the research they are producing is intriguing, complex, and often compelling. Thus, this review focuses on providing a thorough discussion of the components of quality learning over the Web.

Who Is Interested?

A number of parties are interested in having a definition of quality in distance education, including the federal government, accreditors, state regulators, faculty organizations, and students.

Federal Regulators

The U.S. Department of Education has an interest in determining quality for several reasons. Based on the department's concern for quality education, rules established before distance education became a viable way to serve students have precluded distance education students from receiving financial aid. As of this writing, these rules are being revised to be more supportive of distance education students. Additional actions include the department's Distance Education Demonstration Program (to experiment with removing or revising current rules) and creation by the U.S. Congress of the Web-Based Commission, whose final report (2001) supports making changes in policies and rules to encourage the development of more, and better, Web-based learning opportunities.

Accreditors

Accrediting associations have also been forced to grapple with existing definitions of quality and how distance education questions those definitions. In the past, accreditors relied on peer review and traditional measures for quality—largely input and process measures—focusing on procedures, not on what is actually learned. The six regional accrediting associations (New England Association of Schools and Colleges, Middle States Commission on Higher Education, North Central Association–Commission on Institutions of Higher Education, Northwest Association of Schools and Colleges, Southern Association of Colleges and Schools, Western Association of Schools and Colleges), however, adopted a joint *Statement of the Regional Accrediting Commissions on the Evaluation of Electronically Offered Degree and Certificate Programs and Guidelines for the Evaluation of Electronically Offered Degree and Certificate Programs* (Council of Regional Accrediting Commissions, 2000). The guidelines largely support on-line education and recognize its unique characteristics.

The Council for Higher Education Accreditation (1998) correctly identifies quality assurance in distance education as more focused on the client and student learning assessment than on process but belies a preference for traditional quality assurance strategies based on faculty control and the "core purposes of collegiate higher education" (p. xi). Thus, accreditation has become a battlefield between those who would use traditional accrediting standards to forestall the changes wrought by distance education and those who would change accreditation. Unfortunately, as Schweiger (1996) has pointed out, they measure "the very aspects that distance education . . . is designed to overcome." Although traditional measures may be inappropriate for distance education, what will take their place?

Accreditation has become a battlefield between those who would use traditional accrediting standards to forestall the changes wrought by distance education and those who would change accreditation.

State Regulators

States have two roles when it comes to quality of distance education. Depending on the model of higher education governance current in the state, some governing bodies may have a role in overseeing program approval or review of distance programs offered by in-state institutions, public or private. In others, this duty is delegated to the institution, with the state playing a monitoring role or taking no role whatsoever.

In its second role, many states have the responsibility to authorize out-of-state or unaccredited institutions to operate within the state (represented by such organizations as the National Association of State Approving Agencies). These functions are more likely to operate on a consumer protection mandate, protecting the state's residents from fraudulent educational providers and diploma mills. Often, these functions review newly created institutions on traditional quality measures as well as business practices, and thus the lack of accepted criteria or standards for quality distance education also affects their ability to review and approve distance education programs offered by out-of-state providers.

In both these roles, the state oversees or authorizes the programs and universities in the state. Given the difficulty of regulating program delivery and the ubiquitous nature of the Web (which can provide anytime, anywhere education), Kovel-Jarboe (1997) argues that the state should focus on "educating the consumers of higher education" (p. 25) instead.

Faculty

Faculty organizations such as the American Association of University Professors (AAUP), the American Federation of Teachers (AFT), and individual institutional faculty senates and outspoken critics (e.g., David Noble) have also spoken to the issue of quality in distance education. The AAUP has two statements on distance education (2001a, 2001b) that identify the issues of greatest interest to professors, including academic freedom, intellectual property rights, faculty workload, and compensation.

Students

Students also have an interest in what quality is, but the definition may be largely different from those considered by other parties. It may be, if we have not already asked them, that they express their opinions of what is good for them by enrolling and paying tuition. Thus, enrollment patterns may be one way of detecting students' view of quality. On the other hand, many students have difficulty in knowing what quality is and depend on others (e.g., accreditors, the U.S. Department of Education) to guide them.

Impact on Discussions of Quality

Especially in contrast to the legislative point of view, faculty often view the goals of expanding access and lowering cost as a priori proof of decreased quality. Cost equals quality in this model. The new marketplace, with its nontraditional providers and products, is also suspect, as it is unlike what has traditionally been accepted as *quality*. Diverging from the norm is therefore suspect. Opponents use the charge of declining quality as a "codeword for protectionism . . . [and apply] a higher standard to nontraditional delivery systems" (Kovel-Jarboe, 1997, p. 25). Clearly, the different factions have preconceptions that affect their definitions of what quality is or should be. Therefore, any discussion of the research on quality in distance education must deal with these competing views and understand the ways that individual beliefs and perceptions affect one's judgment and interpretation of research.

The discussion of quality is therefore both emotional and influenced by a perception that on-line learning changes power structures as well as traditional roles—affecting some with a fear of loss, a fear that the new structure or role will be difficult to fulfill or be less satisfying, and a fear that the new marketplace could bring irreparable harm to institutions to which individuals have devoted their careers and lives. These emotions are powerful, and they mean that neither is quality a simple concept nor can it be easily argued. Even rational arguments may be motivated or modified by emotional and personal beliefs.

In fact, many discussions of quality are not about quality at all but about basic perceptions and deification of the status quo. That is why a more in-depth and broader review of the factors that may lead to quality distance education is needed, including an attempt to understand emotional as well as theoretical issues. As will become clear, the issues are complex, the field is rapidly changing, and practitioners and researchers alike are constantly improving how on-line learning is conducted.

What Is Ahead

The following review has seven chapters. Chapter Two first describes the early research studies that produced the much discussed and poorly understood "no significant difference phenomenon" and then discusses the critics of that research and research on distance education generally. Chapters Three, Four, and Five describe the research we have and the research questions we need answered. Chapter Three covers several pertinent research issues, Chapter Four research on technology and students, and Chapter Five research on faculty and higher education institutions. These three chapters identify the strands of research that can contribute to a definition of quality that both traditionalists and distance educators can support. Chapter Six takes an important detour through a discussion of current guidelines developed by various bodies, and Chapter Seven provides a summary of advice to individuals and institutions grappling with the complicated issue of quality in on-line learning. Chapter Eight, a set of overarching conclusions, stresses large trends in the research (which regretfully misses some of the more interesting, individual findings from the research). Given how many faculty are conducting research on this topic, it is important to consider some of this material as tentative; criteria for quality will have to evolve as additional studies are completed and their results modify our understanding of how learning occurs over the Web.

The Significance of "No Significance"

T HIS CHAPTER DESCRIBES THE EARLY STUDIES on distance education and the origination of the "no significant difference phenomenon." An understanding of these studies is crucial to appreciating both the history of research on distance education and our current difficulties with research on on-line learning. The critics of this research have their say, and then the critics are in turn the object of criticism. This perspective can help us develop a better understanding of the political and emotional ramifications of research on on-line learning, for proponents and opponents alike.

State of the Art

In this section, the state of the art for distance education research will be reviewed, from the "no significant difference" phenomenon to the more current criticisms of that research.

No Significant Difference Phenomenon

Perhaps the most quoted and misunderstood body of research on distance education has been the work of Russell (1999), who reviewed 355 studies on distance education produced from 1928 to 1998. To a large extent, the studies compared instruction over videotape, interactive video, or satellite, whether telecourses or television, with on-campus, in-person courses. Students were compared on test scores, grades, or performance measures unique to the study as well as student satisfaction. Consistently, based on statistical tests, "no significant difference" between the comparison groups was found.

Only 40 of the 355 studies specifically included computer-based instruction, and the compilation was completed before the blossoming of courses using the Web. Chapter Four focuses on the research on Web-based courses, but it is important to understand the ramifications of Russell's work. Despite the technology used, the results are the same: no difference in student achievement. Russell concludes, "There is nothing inherent in the technologies that elicits improvements in learning," although "the process of redesigning a course to adapt the content to the technology" can improve the course and improve the outcomes (p. xiii). In other words, learning is not caused by the technology but by the instructional method "embedded in the media" (Clark, 1994, p. 22). Technology, then, is "merely a means of delivering instruction," a delivery truck, so to speak, that does not influence achievement. Russell (1999) concludes, "No matter how it is produced, how it is delivered, whether or not it is interactive, low-tech or high-tech, students learn equally well" (p. xiv). After so many studies, Russell expressed his frustration that people continue to believe that technology impacts learning.

Surprisingly, a large number of studies reviewed for this report still compare student achievement between Web-based versus in-person delivery models. Not surprisingly, the results of studies by Bourne, McMaster, Rieger, and Campbell (1997), Davies and Mendenhall (1998), Dominguez and Ridley (1999), Gagne and Shepherd (2001), Hahn and others (1990), Johnson (2001), McNeil and others (1991), Miller (2000), Mulligan and Geary (1999), Ryan (2000), Schulman and Sims (1999), Sener and Stover (2000), Serban (2000), Wegner, Holloway, and Garton (1999), and Wideman and Owston (1999) remain largely the same as in Russell's compilation: comparing the two types of delivery methods leads to a conclusion of no significant difference in student achievement. In all fairness to these studies, however, several found differences in completion or student satisfaction, although final grades or exam scores were often the same, or nearly the same, between the two types of courses compared.

Why Comparison Studies?

What can explain this continued use of a repudiated research design? Are researchers unfamiliar with the work of Clark (1994) or Kozma (1994a, 1994b)?

Have they not read the earlier reviews of research done by Moore and Thompson (1997), Moore and Cozine (2000), Simonson, Smaldino, Albright, and Zvacek (2000), and Gibson (1990)? This is an interesting phenomenon, and although it may be the result of many factors, it may also be an outgrowth of the traditional division between researchers and practitioners, especially when practitioners present their studies without reference to the earlier body of work. Both Sabelli and Dede (2000) and Brown and Johnson-Shull (2000) provide touching analyses of the separation between researchers and practitioners and the "failure of research to inform practice" (G. Brown and Johnson-Shull, 2000).

To return to the issue of comparison studies, what perhaps may be more understandable is that this straightforward comparison may be the faculty person's first foray into evaluating whether the technology works; the study is relatively simple in design, does not match student samples or use control groups, and ignores the need to separate the instructor from the researcher. Despite these flaws, the study is ultimately influential in allaying faculty fears that the experiment is working as well as other more traditional options. This outcome may be the study's most important contribution: helping faculty test the technology for themselves and see the results with their own eyes. If it is motivation for the enduring presence of these types of studies in conferences and on-line journals, then perhaps these comparison studies will continue until all faculty have tested this hypothesis for themselves.

As is discussed in the next section, this relatively simple (one might suggest naive) study design is roundly criticized but may be understandable if it is seen as the right of every faculty person to ask this basic question before investigating more complicated issues. In other words, the prevalence of this study design may be attributable not to ignorance of the large body of work that Russell attempted to highlight or to a need to prove the results for themselves (although this may be a sufficient explanation) but may be seen as a natural and normal first step toward testing whether this new technology is as good as other models.

Multiple Interpretations

Before proceeding to the critics, however, it is important to note the many ways the "no significant differences" research has been interpreted. Some have pointed out that given the high cost of purchasing equipment and building networks, one would expect a higher return on learning to justify such an expense. In this view, the higher cost of technology-supported distance education would preclude further development of courses and programs for results that are "no better than" traditional models. Although this cost argument is important, it has not slowed the growth of distance education, simply because the choice for some students is often between technology-supported distance education or no education at all.

To others, the results indicate support for technology, because it appears to cause no harm while markedly increasing access to higher education. Lockee, Burton, and Cross (1999) make the point that "failure to reject the null hypothesis means just that and nothing more; just as a legal finding of not guilty does not mean innocent" (p. 34). The two methods of instruction are not equally effective (or ineffective), for too much remains unexplained. And that is where the critics come in.

Recent Criticism of the Research

Phipps and Merisotis (1999), in a report on the research into distance education funded by the AFT and the National Education Association (NEA), provided the latest attack on the no significant difference research. Their critique focuses on the lack of those elements that distinguish quality research, such as control groups, randomization of treatment groups, matching of student populations, statistical sophistication, and consistency in treatments (among others). They fault the research for focusing on courses rather than programs, not accounting for differences in students (especially learning styles), the interaction of multiple technologies, and not basing research on theoretical frameworks. They conclude, as did Clark (1994) and Russell (1999) before them, that perhaps the value of technology is that it leads to the question, What is the best way to teach students? But they also conclude that "it seems clear that technology cannot replace the human factor in higher education" (Phipps and Merisotis, 1999, p. 31), a claim that is not substantiated by the research.

Green (in Morrison, 1999) also states that we need to "acknowledge we don't yet have clear, compelling evidence about the impact of information technology on student learning and educational outcomes." Moore and Thompson (1997) had also noted the weak research designs and lack of control elements in the early media comparison studies. More recently, Joy and Garcia (2000), in a meta-analysis of studies comparing technology with traditional delivery modes found poorly designed research that did not control for many important variables. In other words, so much of the early research did not account for the types of complicating variables—student learning styles, maturity, multiple intelligences (to name but a few)—that have since been indicated as important factors in student learning.

And to make the point once again, the American Center for the Study of Distance Education (1999) reviewed articles published in on-line journals and magazines from 1997 to 1999 and found that only 6 of a total of 170 articles employed a quasi-experimental approach. The remainder focused on describing ongoing projects, taking a position on the technology or distance education, or providing evaluation information on the completed project. Berge and Mrozowski (2001) reviewed articles from 1990 to 1999 and found that 84 percent of the research articles were descriptive and case studies; only 7 percent were experimental and 8 percent were correlational research studies. And it continues to be true that the majority of articles published on distance education, Web-based education, and quality continue to be position papers, personal experiences, and advice to others contemplating a Web-based course. These articles may provide excellent advice, but they rarely present the results of well-designed research. Fortunately, this situation is changing, as Chapters Four and Five document.

The Critics Criticized

The critics, however, have come into their share of criticism, most notably from G. Brown and Wack (1999a), who faulted the Phipps and Merisotis (1999) report for being overly simplistic, inequitable with their criticisms (which might also apply to traditional education), inconsistent, contradictory, and holding distance education to a higher burden of proof. What is important in so many reports attacking distance education is the presumption that traditional education (usually poorly defined) is the norm against which comparison must be made and that traditional education is a laudable norm. Unfortunately, using traditional education in this fashion usually generates a list of ways it already fails students: depending on lectures and rote or passive learning, and allowing no (or low) interaction with faculty or other students.

G. Brown and Wack (1999a), however, would also aver that Green's plea for "clear, compelling evidence" assumes that such evidence is attainable and comparisons relevant (and that such evidence is available for the so-called "traditional" course or program). Despite this point, it is important to note that this exchange among critics focuses less on the need for better research (a position universally agreed to) than on the willingness of critics and proponents alike to choose their "evidence" based on their point of view. As discussed previously, two researchers looking at the same evidence (e.g., no significant differences) would interpret its meaning in wildly divergent ways.

What the Critics Reveal

All these critiques of research reveal a number of misunderstandings about research itself. First, the nature of research is that it is a test of a hypothesis, only as good as the theory that generated the hypothesis and the individuals who design and conduct the research. At best, once completed, it may shed some light on the topic being researched; at worst, it may tell us more about the researcher and his or her skills. (And as a reviewer kindly mentioned, statistics require that we conceive of false positives and false negatives, a fact easily forgotten in a society that reifies quantification.) Indeed, there is a long history of poorly done research in education, and in any case, researchers (and their interpreters) are often prone to generalizing beyond the scope of the actual experiment or test. It is very difficult (and perhaps impossible) to control all of the variables in a study, let alone a study dealing with human beings. In all deference to the researchers who struggle to unravel how humans learn, however, it is no easy task.

Second, it is perhaps obvious by now to note that researchers, compilers of research, and interpreters of research are influenced by their values and beliefs and often see only what they are looking for. Research can and does follow political and other agendas and its claim as truth regularly impugned by others with different agendas or beliefs. Since the work of Gould (1981), among others, researchers are recognized as humans, subject to failures in self-knowledge and objectivity. Especially when the topic is distance education, where the stakes are large and fears may affect one's judgment, research must take into account the larger environmental context of the researcher and especially his/her beliefs and assumptions about education and distance education (see especially G. Brown and Wack, 1999a).

As this review proceeds to a look at the recent research on Web-based distance education, it is well to remember that human beliefs (of the researcher, the author, and the reader) can complicate the original design of the research and our understanding of the results as well as any interpretation made of the implications drawn from the results. You may well conclude that the research on distance education is confused (that is true), and you may find anything you want to find (also true). But this is a good argument for tackling the sort of research that can incorporate more complicated relationships and concepts and expand our understanding of what is really affecting student learning in a Web-based course.

Last, what this argument between critics also reveals is that the use of technology is a bellwether for many, one that creates an emotional—perhaps visceral—response on the part of those who fear technology and as emotional a response from those who thrill at discovering new ways of doing things. What is lost in this to-and-fro argument is an understanding of the impact of how the Web may best be used in a class rather than arguing over whether it should be used at all. In other words, as the following chapters reveal, the Web presents faculty with choices on how to use it, and as such, its effectiveness may be more the result of those choices than the characteristics of the Web itself. Or to put it even more bluntly, it is irrelevant to speak of the effects of using the Web without understanding how it is entwined with instructional design and especially faculty choices about instructional design. What is disheartening about this insight is that so many

It is irrelevant to speak of the effects of using the Web without understanding how it is entwined with instructional design and especially faculty choices about instructional design.

earlier researchers came to this same conclusion, yet many current studies seem unaware of this body of work. Current advocates and opponents to using the Web must understand this point to be able to design the sort of useful research that will help improve students' educational experiences.

Summary

It is important to understand the history of research on distance education, the significance of the no significant difference phenomenon, and the various ways the phenomenon has been interpreted. The critics of this research and the critics of the critics have played out their perceptions and beliefs in the literature as well, leading one to conclude that the discussion of research on quality is plagued with personal and political agendas. This insight is useful as this review proceeds, which turns next to a short discussion on research design, definitions, and theories appropriate for on-line learning.

Research Basics

THIS CHAPTER FOCUSES on some important issues for conducting and understanding research on on-line learning. It introduces the reader to the sources for studies included in this review, many of which are available on-line. It stresses the importance of balance, the avoidance of "absolutes," the difficulty of defining quality in light of the complex nature of learning. It concludes with a discussion of useful theoretical approaches for research on on-line learning, including constructivism, multiple intelligences, and cognitive theory.

Source of Studies

This review drew on research literature in ERIC, compiled by the American Center for the Study of Distance Education, as well as relevant Web sites (e.g., Center for Knowledge Communication, Institute for Learning Technologies, Institute for Computer-Based Learning, among others), on-line journals (e.g., *The Technology Source, T.H.E. Journal, Ed at a Distance, The Online Journal of Distance Learning Administration, International Review of Research on Open and Distance Learning, the Journal of Asynchronous Learning Networks,* among others), conference sites (e.g., Teaching in the Community Colleges Online Conference, the Australian World Wide Web Conference), and listservs (e.g., DEOS, WCETALL, The Learning Marketplace).

Fortunately, the Web is increasingly home to reports and papers that are posted to a Web site and available to all, so those who seek information about the research faculty are pursuing need only review some of these fine sites.

Unfortunately, there are a lot of studies (some more amateur than others), some may not have successfully passed through traditional forms of peer review, and many others certainly seem eminently publishable and worth reviewing. This use of the Web may spell a diminishment in the importance of journal publications, or it may augment traditional journals with papers that are more accessible to more people and provide greater visibility for the author and his or her ideas. Like much with the Web, we need to wait and see.

Absolutes

This literature review attempts to fairly depict the research results and delineate the pros and cons (and unknowns) of using the Web in distance education or on-campus courses. Absolutism, or the preference for sweeping statements that on-line learning is all good or all bad, is not productive, nor is the interpretation of research results for the cause of supporting or defeating distance education. Therefore, the aim of this review is to better understand how the Web supports learning well (or not), which students may (or may not) learn well on-line, and which faculty and institutions may (or may not) succeed in this environment.

Definitional Dragons

If one problem makes research into quality most difficult, it is the lack of consistent, agreed-on definitions for what quality is. "I will know it when I see it" does not work. This task is not simple, however, as the definition of quality is personal and based on past formative experiences ("when I was in college"), assumptions (face-to-face interaction is best), and values (education is for the whole person, not just preparation for work). It is tied inextricably to entrenched views of what higher education is and ought to do, from producing graduates who can perform on the job, be able and constructive citizens, and be discriminating intellectuals.

But the problems of useful definitions do not end there. Ehrmann (1997) makes a good point when he decries the use of the term *traditional education* when it is used to refer to a higher education that is neither uniform nor stable.

This is an important criticism of many comparison studies, reviewed in Chapter Two, as well as writers who speak of *traditional education* without defining it. Distance education is equally difficult to define, what with Web-based or -enhanced courses, and there are no clear and consistent definitions of what they might be.

Similar problems affect a definition of quality. As Oblinger (1998) asked, Is quality assessed based on faculty expertise or volumes in the library? Are some criteria more important than others? Further, how much weight should be placed on the traditional input variables, i.e., faculty degree or rank, library volumes, number and variety of degree programs, Carnegie classification. Which process variables should we use, those dealing with instructional models, attention to student learning styles and other important differences, the use made of technology, faculty/student ratios or class size, contact hours, or opportunities to be taught by full professors? And what outcome variables indicate quality—the final GPA, student satisfaction, alumni giving, or some assessment of what has been learned (if possible)?

This discussion is important for several reasons, perhaps the most important being the realization that some of the input and process variables that have marked a quality education in the past (e.g., library volumes or contact hours) are precisely those variables distance education makes less necessary than before or eliminates entirely. Thus, as definitions for quality education are applied to distance education, we should not be surprised that sometimes the results are skewed in favor of the earlier form and present distance education in a poorer light. Having said this, however, does not preempt the responsibility of those in distance education to derive its own definitions of quality—whether input, process, or outcome—and the research basis upon which such a definition can be supported. The chapter "Advice to the Confused" may help in that regard.

Complexity of Research on Learning

To produce useful results, research must account for a variety of influences on what is being studied. Learning is especially complex and conducting good research on learning therefore especially demanding. The problem with most research studies on learning is the difficulty of isolating factors so that their impact (if any) can be identified and understood, separate from the action of other factors in the environment. Unfortunately for researchers, learning is both complex and occurs in very rich environments. It is doubly difficult to unravel influences from the individual's personality, values, brain, background (family, school, friends, work), and, of course, the educational environment (classroom, teacher acts, pedagogical choices, tools).

The challenge of studying a complex act in a complicated environment also applies to studies of technology-based learning, making it very difficult to get answers to such questions as, for instance, does the Web work best only with persons with visual-spatial intelligence? Or, does technology interact in some fashion with learning styles to make one learning style better with Web-based courses, or can the introverted student learn to collaborate with one technology better than another? Given this fundamental problem, clear and definitive answers from research will likely be beyond the state of the art as it exists today.

Theoretical Approaches

Among the learning theories that have guided higher education, perhaps constructivism, the theory of multiple intelligences, and the cognitive theory of multimedia learning have the greatest likelihood of informing Web-based distance education practice. They seem especially appropriate for adults as well as traditional-age college students.

Constructivism is based on the belief and evidence that learners "actively construct knowledge in their attempts to make sense of their world" (see Murphy, 1997, for an excellent review). This constructivism suggests that the mind works by making sense, relating new information to prior knowledge and experience, and interacting with the world (Diaz, 2000; Murphy, 1997). It is in contrast to objectivism, which supposes that reality is preexisting and is external to the student, who must discover it. Instructivism posits that learning occurs when information is successfully transferred from a knowledgeable authority figure to the learner. Behaviorism presupposes that the student's mind is a tabula rasa, to be directed or filled by the teacher. Objectivism, instructivism, and behaviorism portray the learner as relatively passive and the role of education as "knowledge transfer"; each is also fairly instructor-centric. Thus, the movement in popularity from objectivism to constructivism has been portrayed as a movement from a "static, passive view of knowledge toward a more adaptive and active view" (Heylighen in Murphy, 1997). It corresponds to a movement from a more passive role to a more active one for the learner, and a concomitant change for faculty from a role as knowledge holder and provider to one as a facilitator and guide to students' learning.

Diaz (2000) has noted this correlation between constructivist models and the transition from teacher-centered to learner-centered education, as detailed by Barr and Tagg (1995). B. Brown (1998) and others have noted the fortunate alignment of the rise in constructivist-based education with the advent of the Web, with the Web facilitating the opportunity for students to make connections, construct meaning, navigate, and create their own knowledge. In this view, learning is self-directed (following the student's natural interests and motivations) as well as collaborative (more on this in the discussion on interaction). The work of J. Brown (2000) has led to insights into how groups create and share knowledge, thereby developing a model of distributed intelligence where knowledge is distributed across individuals and groups in the workplace. Burbules and Callister (2000) call the Internet a *working space* within which knowledge can be co-constructed, negotiated, and revised over time . . . where communities of inquiry can grow and thrive."

Similar to and rooted in constructivism is contextual learning, which focuses on helping students make connections between what they are learning and how it will be used. In contextual learning theory, learning occurs only when students (learners) "process new information or knowledge in such a way that it makes sense to them in their own frames of reference (their own inner worlds of memory, experience, and response)" (Center for Occupational Research and Development, 2001). Contextual learning focuses on problem solving, provides multiple contexts for learning, helps students monitor their learning so they can be self-regulating learners, encourages them to learn from each other, and uses authentic assessment (Berns and Erickson, 2001; Imel, 2000).

Experiential learning is also well adapted to Web-based environments. Pimentel (1999) has found some support that a virtual environment can be effective for creating the conditions for experiential learning. Work by Bleck (1999, 2000) seems to support this assertion. Bleck (2000) agrees with Dewey's claim that "all genuine education comes about through experience" if that experience modifies the one who is acting, which is a real possibility in the environment Bleck describes. Dede (1996) also supports this idea and underscores the ability of Web-based learning to create simulation systems that help students construct knowledge.

With constructivism also comes an appreciation for knowledge having multiple interpretations, mirroring the complexity of the real world and the people in it. The real world also generates and provides an environment for authentic tasks for learners, where errors may be more educational and apt to generate revisions of prior learning and perceptions than rote learning. Problem-based learning creates active forms of learning that have been proved to positively change prior beliefs and inadequate or wrong mental models (see Marchese, 2000), which in other situations are quite impervious to change.

Another justification for authentic, problem-based learning is the pursuit of *transformative learning* (see Mezirow, 1991). Learners are transformed when they encounter "disorienting dilemmas," dilemmas that help learners assess their earlier beliefs and begin the process of changing them. By moving students from a passive to a more active role, on-line learning can create disorientation, encourage reflection, and help transform students' learning and themselves (Sawyer and O'Fallon, 2000).

The Web can be instrumental in creating complex worlds (or providing access to real complex worlds), allowing students to work together to understand and solve real-world problems and grasp the multiplicity of viewpoints and interpretations that others may have. Research by Garrison (1999) supports the ability of project-based learning in a Web class to produce exceptional learning, despite problems with learning via the new technology.

Constructivism may be a theory especially appropriate for adult students, based on Knowles's andragogy (1978), or theory of how adults learn. Andragogy assumes that adults become more self-directing over time, their personal experiences affect learning, their readiness to learn is based on environment and events in the adult's life, and they have a problem-centered orientation to learning. Similarities to constructivism are obvious. Constructivism may also be a theory for our times, as its similarity to postmodern thinking (see Wilson, 1997) is striking. Both emphasize a plurality of perspectives and meanings, an appreciation of alternative interpretations, and acknowledgement of multiple truths.

Gardner (1983) first proposed the concept of *multiple intelligences* in learners and has extended the application of multiple intelligences in several works. The eight learning intelligences are (1) logico-mathematical, people who learn best through the manipulation of numbers, logic, and syllogisms; (2) verbal-linguistic, people who learn best through manipulating words and concepts; (3) musical, people who learn aurally and can interpret cultural implications of music; (4) visual-spatial, people who learn through or with aesthetic qualities; (5) kinesthetic, people who learn best by participating tactually; (6) interpersonal, people who learn best through personal interactions with others; (7) intrapersonal, people who favor personal, reflective learning; (8) naturalist, people who recognize large, overarching patterns in nature.

Gen (2000) proposes that technology is "a way to allow the utilization of various intelligences" with software (spreadsheet analysis for the logico-mathematicals) or projects (collaborative teams for the interpersonals) tailored to the strengths of students or offered to improve weak intelligences. Nelson (1998) also provides suggestions for the use of tools and activities offered by the Web in light of the theory of multiple intelligences. Thus, the different modes of learning made possible by the Internet could also provide a fruitful area for insights into quality. And although verbal-analytic intelligence has been the usual way that students succeed in academe, increasing evidence suggests that visual-spatial intelligence will be most useful in dealing with Web-based environments. And as Healy (1999) suggests, the visual-spatial intelligence may be most highly developed in the young students arriving at higher education's doors after years of experiencing multimedia and video games. As the reader will come to realize, very little research has been done that looks specifically at multiple intelligences and on-line learning.

A third theory that may be very useful in understanding and evaluating Web-based learning comes from *cognitive theory* in the field of multimedia learning. The relationship of multimedia learning to the Web is not so far removed as one might expect, as both use visual, auditory, and text-based communications. Mayer (2001) presumes that for meaningful learning to occur, the learner must use five cognitive processes: (1) selecting relevant words for processing in verbal working memory, (2) selecting relevant images for processing in visual working memory, (3) organizing words into a verbal mental model, (4) organizing images into a visual mental model, and (5) integrating verbal and visual representations (p. 54). Mayer also proposes seven design principles that have been proved to help students learn better: (1) using words and pictures rather than words alone, (2) presenting corresponding words and pictures near to rather than far from each other, (3) presenting corresponding words and pictures simultaneously, (4) excluding extraneous words, pictures, and sounds, (5) using animation and narration rather than animation and on-screen text, (6) using animation and narration rather than animation, narration, and on-screen text, and (7) using the design principles for low-knowledge and spatial learners. Readers interested in the principles, the limits on cognitive processes that form the basis of the principles, and the tests conducted on the principles should review Mayer (2001, pp. 185–196). Research on applying this perspective to on-line learning would be welcome.

Summary

This chapter has focused on research basics for conducting research on on-line learning. It is clear from this short review that we lack a definition of quality, which makes it difficult to discuss quality without clarifying what is meant or implied by the term. What is also clear is the difficulty of designing good research on such a complex act as learning. But fortunately, several theoretical approaches seem to be especially appropriate for research on on-line learning, including constructivism, multiple intelligences, and cognitive theory for multimedia learning.

Research on Technology and Students

THIS CHAPTER FOCUSES ON DESCRIBING the research on use of the Web and the role of students on the creation of quality education experiences in on-line courses or programs. The role of Web technology focuses on its ability to support a variety of pedagogies and the results from several comparison studies as well as case studies. Its greatest importance, however, may be its ability to support ample interaction between and among students, faculty, and course material and the development of learning communities. Of course, a fair review must include the fears most frequently heard about technology use as well as some intriguing research on how humans mistake technology for reality.

The role of the learner focuses on the individual characteristics of learners—from motivation to attitude, preparation, gender, and various learning styles—and their influence on successful on-line learning, including improved critical thinking and writing skills. The last sections review two areas of research that are especially intriguing (although not definitive): the impact Web use may have on the human spirit and brain development.

The Role of Technology

It may seem odd to begin a review of research by focusing first on the role of technology when so much has been written that questions the effect of technology on learning. This discussion is placed early in the research review because many readers may still believe that technology does have an independent impact on learning. Whether it has such an effect, and why that may or not be so, is the topic of the next section.

Pedagogy and Technology

If the comparison studies (Russell, 1999) accomplished anything, they established that the technology studied did not make as much difference in the selected learning outcomes as some expected—because interactive video (two-way audio and videoconferencing) may sufficiently duplicate the traditional classroom teacher-centered model as to be indistinguishable from that model. Its instructional model is *one-to-many*, whether delivered in person through a lecture, television, or interactive video. Or as Morrison (2001) remarked, "If you try to compare media, you have to keep the instruction constant. If you keep it constant, and the medium does not change the message/instruction, you will find no significant difference."

> **If the comparison studies accomplished anything, they established that the technology studied did not make as much difference in the selected learning outcomes as some expected.**

Although many aspects of using the Web have been investigated, other issues have not. Research is needed into the usefulness or appropriateness of the Web for different disciplines or learning objectives. Fahy (2000) calls it "technology's fitness for use" as a teaching tool and asks—as others have—whether the technology is directly related to the learning outcome. Are some technologies more appropriate for visually based disciplines and others better for discourse, as Tuckey (1993) contends? Is the Web good for lower-division courses but inadequate for graduate seminars? And what is the "best media mix" to achieve different learning goals? (Harasim and others, 1996). Or, as Burbules and Callister (2000) put the challenge, *"Which* technologies have educational potential for *which* students, for *which* subject matters, and for *which* purposes?" Or is Russell correct and the Internet no different from a delivery truck?

An answer may be emerging to the series of "which" questions posed by Burbules and Callister. In early studies of K–12 students studying science reviewed by Helgeson (1988), the most effective combination of instructional opportunities included hands-on laboratory experiences and computer simulations, improving students' scientific thinking. This study is one of the first that drew attention to the possibility that a mix of media may be the most powerful means of education. Campos and Harasim (1999) found 55 percent of students prefer mixed-mode classes: those that combine face-to-face and on-line activities. Young (2002) describes "hybrid" teaching (or the "the convergence of on-line and resident instruction") at several universities, which one university president calls "the single-greatest unrecognized trend in higher education today." Dziuban and Moskal (2001) found that courses with both a Web and face-to-face component produced the same or better success rates than courses that were fully on-line or face-to-face. This result teases us into asking whether there is some optimal combination of technologies—not limited to face-to-face, interactive video, and Web—that maximize learning based on the needs of the curriculum, the type of learning desired, and the learner's characteristics. Over time, the correct question to ask may not be which is better but what combination is best.

More Comparison Studies

Several studies compare students' success or experiences in on-line courses to traditional courses. (One can see these studies as continuing the tradition of comparison studies as reviewed by Russell [1999].) Schutte (1997) found that his on-line students earned 37 more points (out of 200) than his face-to-face students, even though the on-line students were not substantially different from the other students. Paskey (2001) reports on a study at Athabasca University that found on-line students "experienced greater cognitive and explanatory learning" as a result of greater participation in course communications where students exchange "between 80 to 100 messages, which is far richer than the classroom." Parker and Gemino (2001) did not find significant differences in student performance but did find that on-line students scored higher in conceptual learning and that face-to-face students scored higher in learning the application of techniques. Benbunan-Fich, Hiltz, and Turoff (2001) compared face-to-face and asynchronous learning groups as they worked on case studies; the on-line group had broader discussions and submitted more complete reports, while the face-to-face group worked the problem sequentially.

Tucker (2001) found significant differences in students' posttest scores, final exam scores, and age (in favor of the distance students) but no significant differences in pretest scores and grades given for homework, research papers, and the course. Such studies hint at the complexity of comparing courses and unraveling the factors impacting students' achievement on-line and on campus.

Hartman, Dziuban, and Moskal (2000), in a study of asynchronous learning network (ALN) courses matched with traditional counterparts found that ALN courses produced lower withdrawal rates and higher success rates. In Hiltz's study of ALNs (1997), students were more likely to delay and procrastinate, which may be a quality of the student or the asynchronous design of the course, or a lack of proactive behavior on the part of the faculty. Yet the students felt they worked harder, had greater access to the professor, and appreciated the convenience of the medium; the percentage of As and Bs given also increased. And in research reviewed by B. Brown (2000) comparing Web-based versus traditional classroom interactions, the on-line students felt they achieved a greater depth of understanding and had a greater ability to participate in discussions, although they also felt more disconnected from others and experienced more technical problems (which may explain the feelings of disconnection). Navarro and Shoemaker (2000) compared cyberlearners with traditional learners and found that the cyberlearners learn as well or better than traditional learners, regardless of gender, ethnicity, academic background, and computer skills.

Case Studies and Others

The following discussion focuses on results from case studies and other research designs that may or may not compare Web-based education with other modes but that have found a variety of positive outcomes to using the Web in the delivery and/or enhancement of the course. Fitzsimmons and O'Brien (2000), in a case study of teaching an on-line course, found higher pass rates than when the course was offered in traditional mode and found the format useful for understanding students' own learning modalities, becoming aware of the "processes of their learning as distinct from the content of learning to improve their learning outcomes." Gibson and Rutherford (2000) describe extensive use of Web-based communications to "create a sense of group experience" and develop community among students in the course. Jones's case study (1996) of on-line learning identified students as "cyberspace natives" or as "immigrants," who required additional training to succeed. The author also concludes, "you can't please all of the people," because students have different tastes, backgrounds, learning styles, network connections, and Web browsers. Edelson (2000) found that on-line students reported a greater sense of community than in face-to-face courses; face-to-face courses can potentially create a "coercive environment" where students feel manipulated and embarrassed and where they expect the faculty to do all the work.

Sener (2001) also studied ALNs at a community college and found improved student success rates and strong student satisfaction with the courses. Shea and others (2001) also studied ALNs and found almost 80 percent of participating students agreed with the statement that "I learned a great deal in my on-line course." Almost 50 percent indicated they participated more than in regular classrooms, which contributed to a strong correlation between interaction with the instructor and student satisfaction. The quality of interaction was most influenced by "social presence," self-disclosure, and accessibility, with females feeling as though they interacted more and at higher levels than in their other classes.

Two studies are distinguished for their use of control variables. Kuh and Vesper (1999) analyzed data on 125,224 undergraduates and found that, to the extent students became familiar with computers, there was a significant and positive association with self-reported gains in self-directed learning, writing, and problem solving (this study is unique for also having controlled for such factors as grades, age, gender, parental education, and educational aspirations). Another study by Flowers, Pascarella, and Pierson (2000) modeled on the Kuh and Vesper research focused on cognitive impacts of computer use during the first year of college. These results did not duplicate the positive results of Kuh and Vesper (1999), and although the impact on students at four-year colleges was nonsignificant, the results for community college students were positive, indicating a difference in the type of student enrolled in the two settings or their experiences while enrolled. Positive results were found for use of word processing in reading comprehension.

Interaction with Material, Students, and Faculty

The Web's ability to support interaction and collaboration is an important characteristic of the medium as it is used in distance education; this characteristic has received considerable attention. Web use has grown in part because it allows unprecedented interaction between and among students and students, faculty and students, and students with numerous sources of content material. Priest (in Morrison, 2000) has noted that "virtually all of the interactions that are possible in a live classroom environment are replicable in the Internet environment. In fact, in some ways, the interactivity is more powerful. Students can interact with other students via threaded interaction even if they cannot be available at precisely the same time. Students can interact with students who are geographically remote. Neither of these is possible in a traditional environment" (p. 2).

Trentin (2000) suggests a "strict link between quality and the capability to manage a learning process based on the active participation of all" is necessary (p. 18). Wild and Omari (1996) also focus on designing learning environments for the Web that create a conversational framework that allows students to gain access to content, act on that content, gain feedback on their understanding of the content, and adapt the Web materials resulting from reflection. The authors note that they are characteristics not of the Web but of instructional design, which uses only what the Web makes possible. This point is confirmed by Vrasidas and McIsaac (1999), who found that structure of the course, class size, and feedback influenced the amount and type of interaction in the class. (Individuals interested in a rubric for assessing interaction in a Web-based course should see Roblyer and Ekhaml [2000].)

Harasim (1987), in a study comparing graduate-level courses, found seven advantages, the first two referring to increased interaction (quantity and intensity) and access to group knowledge and support (important for the discussion on developing community). Muirhead's review (2001) of the research on interactivity in on-line courses seems to indicate that courses designed to be text-based (largely passive experiences for students) were rated low for interactivity but that courses where participation and feedback occurred between and among faculty and students were ranked much higher. Other advantages of on-line interaction were the ability to reflect on responses and the flexibility to interact when schedules permitted, although timeliness and relevance of responses were also important. Students by and large want to make genuine connections with others, creating a "reciprocal, co-evolutionary relationship" (G. Brown and Wack, 1999b, p. 2) that just happens to occur online. Interaction in the Web-based course can offset social isolation and support a student's natural tendency to connect—but only if the course is designed to take advantage of the medium's capabilities.

This social element was also studied by Wegerif (1998), whose study of ALNs found the ALN model to increase interaction, self-discipline, a sense of community, communication, reflection, and shared space among students. In Hillman's study (1999) of interaction patterns in two types of courses, interaction in the computer-mediated courses resembled discussion, while the face-to-face courses were more like recitation. In all honesty, however, the type of interaction encouraged may have been the result of faculty choices and instructional design rather than the delivery method.

Questions remain about what types of on-line interaction produce meaningful insights for students. Is the effect of interaction idiosyncratic to the person, or is there some type of interaction that engenders more learning from a student? Is there an optimal amount of interaction between and among the faculty, students, and content, and does technology enable or change the quality of interaction?

It is important to grasp the downside of on-line interaction as well. Shell (1994c) has noted that it loses important information, or "richness," including facial expressions, voice intonations, and gestures; jokes and irony can be lost and lead to misunderstandings. And because people cannot see or may not know others personally, they may feel more free to make hurtful or inflammatory remarks. Some individuals may be too worried about their writing skills or worry about who sees their comments. Whether these shortcomings of on-line interaction create permanent or temporary distress and whether or how they are overcome will need to be researched.

Collaboration and On-line Learning Communities

Collaboration, the result of interaction, looks at the give-and-take of on-line communications and focuses on how collaboration supports learning. Hiltz,

Coppola, Trotter, and Turoff (2000) found that collaborative projects resulted in outcomes "as good as or better than those for traditional classes." In an investigation of the key elements that contribute to collaborative learning, Noakes (1999) identified three main qualities (among others), including individual commitment, reciprocity, and group identity, leading to shared or cocreated understandings, sharing of individual competencies, mutual respect and trust, and shared goals.

In an extensive study of asynchronous electronic conferencing at eight universities, Campos, Laferrière, and Harasim (2001) developed a model of "pedagogical-action clusters" by level of collaboration. Figure 1 is an adaptation of their work.

With interaction and collaboration comes the development of community, a concept above and beyond that implied by either of the preceding terms. The question whether there can be community in cyberspace has been answered largely in the affirmative, especially if the on-line course provides the opportunity and the means to do so. Palloff and Pratt (1999) focus on

FIGURE 1
Pedagogical-Action Clusters According to Levels of Collaboration

INDIVIDUAL ACTIVITIES

Network-enhanced lectures

Theme development, text structuring, and case studies

Stand-alone specific activities

Network-enhanced teaching practica

Network-enhanced seminars

Simulation activities

Collaborative learning projects

COLLABORATIVE ACTIVITIES

SOURCE: Campos, Laferrière, and Harasim, 2001.

how community may be defined and created on-line, equating communication with attempts to form community. Wilson and Ryder (2001) define a learning community as one where learners assume and share more control over goals, content, and methods, leading to higher commitment to generating and sharing new knowledge, higher levels of dialogue and collaboration, and a shared project that brings a common focus and incentive to work together. Positive outcomes include greater ability to adapt to conditions and cross traditional boundaries, greater creativity and appreciation for multiple perspectives, and greater personal responsibility to meeting their own and others' learning needs. Negative outcomes to such a learning community include greater inefficiencies and a lack of central control or predictability.

Harasim (in Palloff and Pratt, 1999) has stated that the words *"community* and *communicate* have the same root, *communicare,* which means to share"; people "naturally gravitate toward media that enable us to communicate and form communities because that, in fact, makes us more human" (p. 25). Harasim is quoted by Shell (1994b) as saying that "the Internet is more like a community"; in other words, it is a place, not a highway.

On-line communities suffer some of the same problems of face-to-face communities, including misunderstandings and conflict resulting from a lack of visual/body cues, inability to progress through developmental stages, and lack of constraint by some on-line members. The forging of relationships— once thought to be impossible using an "impersonal" technology—has occurred. Palloff and Pratt (1999) conclude, "The learning community is the vehicle through which learning occurs on-line" (p. 29). Developing community must therefore be pursued as consciously as the course content is explored, requiring shared goals and focused outcomes, interaction and feedback focused toward actively creating knowledge, mutual development of guidelines, and buy-in by participants. Figure 2 is Palloff and Pratt's depiction (1999) of the framework for developing community in distance education courses. Enomoto and Tabata (2000) also found that social bonding and simple information exchange were crucial to creating a virtual learning community, with students supporting and responding to each other, making the course "a student-directed, peer-learning experience."

FIGURE 2
Framework for Building Community in Distance Learning

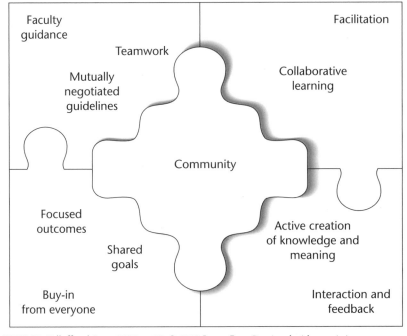

SOURCE: Palloff and Pratt, 1999, p. 30. © 1999 Jossey-Bass. Reprinted with permission.

R. Brown (2001) describes a three-stage process by which community was formed in a computer-mediated asynchronous distance learning class. Stage 1 included making friends (or relationships based on feeling comfortable communicating). Stage 2 was "community conferment" or "acceptance [that] occurred when students were part of a long, thoughtful, threaded discussion on a subject of importance after which participants felt both personal satisfaction and kinship." Stage 3 was camaraderie, which occurred after long-term or intense association that also involved personal communication. Each stage represents a greater degree of engagement "in both the class and the dialogue" over the previous stages. The consequences for students of building community included improved confidence expressing oneself, learning from others, and feeling connected and accepted.

It is fair to conclude that one thing the Web does well is give faculty and students the tools to interact, collaborate, and form learning communities. What determines whether it occurs is whether the course is designed to take advantage of the tools woven into the Web. Put another way, Kozma (1994b) argues that a "distinction must be made between . . . [the] capability of a medium and the variability of its use" (p. 13); in other words, the Web allows for interaction, but the use of this capability is the prerogative of the faculty and the students.

> **The Web allows for interaction, but the use of this capability is the prerogative of the faculty and the students.**

The McLuhan Factor

Marshall McLuhan (1964) proposed the notion that technology is not without its own effects, an idea that has been popularized in the saying "the medium is the message." No question of the effectiveness of distance learning should ignore the impact—intended or not—the Web may have on the learning experience of students or the students themselves. If a particular technology changes learning or the learner, then researchers should be looking for such an impact and assessing its unintended consequences. Yet Levinson (2001), whose analysis of McLuhan's impact on our current understanding of technology is insightful, regrets that McLuhan has fueled "the fire of worry that bad things are happening that we can't know or understand" (p. 19). And although McLuhan's proposition that the "medium has an impact above and beyond what we do with it" (Levinson, 2001, p. 4), evidence is scant that the worriers are correct.

Not surprisingly, however, some writers have concluded that some effects of using the Web are different from the content or instructional model used in the design of the course. An example of this point of view is Slay (1999), who notes that "forms of delivery are not neutral—they invoke or evoke particular kinds of learning behaviour"—and generated a table of qualities that graduates would be expected to develop with use of the Web, including operating on a body of knowledge, preparation for lifelong learning, problem solving, communicating effectively, and working autonomously or collaboratively.

It seems highly likely, however, that the effects of using the Web are entangled with the instructional design. Imel (1999) notes that technologies are not neutral tools; the choices made about which technologies to use as well as how to use them reflect educators' values for relationships with learners and for certain learning models. Disentangling them from the technology itself may be impossible. Morrison (2001) is more blunt: "It is the instructional strategy, not the medium, that makes a difference."

But there are critics. Farber (1998) finds the computer screen to be isolating and decontextualizing, reducing the amount of information available (compared with live situations) and mediating students' experience of reality. The screen, in this view, provides an unbreachable ontological barrier to unmediated experience, or, more simply, it is always virtual and never real, however real the emotions felt by the student. Talbott (1995) also notes that computers shape our thinking by our adapting to the tool, becoming a different personality when "[composing] an electronic mail message [from writing] a note on stationery." And just as the clock transformed our sense of time and the steam engine our sense of distance, the computer reduces human experience to an "abstraction" and solidifies human dependence on machinery and the persons and businesses who promote the new, technical way of entertaining and educating ourselves. And although evidence for these charges is unclear, that does not mean the fears and charges are not valid, only that further research must be done.

Harasim's work (1989) on Internet addiction focuses on the characteristics of the on-line experience that are especially attractive: its visual attractions, its rapid changes that keep the eye tied to the screen, and its opportunities for on-line relationships. Turkle's work (1995) on constructed identities in on-line environments focuses on the Internet's ability to grant users anonymity (or a new persona) if they wish it; with a false identity comes other dangers, although this phenomenon is less likely to occur in ongoing college-level courses. Another crucial aspect to the Internet is its ability to give equal presence (time on screen and even a sense of "officialness") to both quality information and more debatable individual perspectives. As a medium, it has heightened interest in educating students on how to evaluate information found on the Web, similar to Kapinus's list of questions (2001) about the Web site focusing on authority, accuracy, timeliness, and objectivity.

Levinson (2001) asserts that many aspects of McLuhan's thinking have been proved true, including such unintended consequences of using the Internet as the leveling of hierarchy and a diminishment in the role of traditional gatekeepers to knowledge (e.g., universities, libraries). Whether humans are products of media or control media is a significant debate, however, one that philosophers can and do argue either way.

On the opposite side are the proponents who argue that technology is a lever or tool to support the "seven principles of good practice" (Chickering and Ehrmann, 1996). (Indeed, Graham and others [2001] use the seven principles to evaluate four on-line courses to good effect.) This view has several proponents, including Gardner (2000), who supports using technology as a means to a stimulating education rather than as an end in itself. "Technology is a tool; by itself, it cannot teach anything" (Morrison, 2000). Moreover, "technology will never influence anything" (Clark, 1994, p. 21). And although Chapter Two spent substantial space on Clark's assertion, it would be unconscionable to ignore McLuhan's warning. For this is an interesting and crucial difference of opinions between McLuhan and Clark, between seeing technology as a tool that shapes its user and a tool with no or little influence on those who use it. Future researchers into Internet-based education should be watching for secondary and tertiary results that may not become evident until sufficient experience is gained with the medium.

Technology as Reality

There may be an answer to this quandary in the work of Reeves and Nass (1996). In a review of thirty-five studies on how people interact with computers, the authors found that subjects continued to respond to computers as though the computers were real people and places. Their conclusion—that media equal real life—is founded on testing individuals' responses, even going so far as tapping into brain functions as the conscious and rational explanations were at odds with what people did or reasoned.

Reeves and Nass (1996) conclude that it is the psychology of the relationship that is important, not the technology. When asked to critique the computer's work, subjects are "polite"; when asked by a different computer to critique another computer's work, subjects are more likely to offer criticism. Asked to explain their behavior, subjects "know" the difference between a computer and a person and may argue vehemently that technology is a mere tool and certainly without feelings. Yet their responses belie an underlying belief that the computer is real, implying that the relationship of humans to media may be unconscious and perhaps innate. This relationship may be because of, the authors hypothesize, the brain's slow evolution over the ages and its inability to distinguish between rapidly advancing media and real life.

If humans cannot distinguish between computers and real persons, then it would imply that technology does not influence the quality or quantity of learning. It would also argue that failures of learning may the result of faculty skill or instructional design (a discussion developed further in the section on faculty below). It might also argue that "virtual" education—in the sense of something that is not real—is a misnomer that implies an inaccurate message to learners and higher education institutions alike.

The Role of the Learner

This section reviews research that highlights qualities of the learner and how those qualities may impact his or her success at Web-based learning, from personal qualities to learning styles and gender, among others.

Personal Qualities

A number of studies have detailed the importance of such personal qualities as motivation, independence, and self-sufficiency as a learner, and of the goal of earning a degree on the learners' success with distance education (Bernt and Bugbee, 1993; Biner, Bink, Huffman, and Dean, 1995; Fjortoff, 1995). An introvert is more successful in an on-line learning environment, although the student's "academic self-concept" and motivation, previous academic performance, student expectations, and task orientation are also important for success (Gibson, 1997). Self-directedness and computer self-efficacy have been found to be important for student satisfaction with on-line learning (Lim, 2001). In fact, many of the variables that have spelled success for distance learners using earlier modes (e.g., correspondence study, interactive video) may still contribute to success with on-line learning. Lack of confidence (Mabrito, 1998) also impacts students' willingness and ability to interact on-line, crucial to the success of any student participating in on-line discussions and crucial to cognitive development and participation in group projects. Similarly, Bures, Abrami, and Amundsen (2000) found that students who believed that computer conferencing would help them learn and that they were capable of learning on-line were more likely to express satisfaction with the course and to be active on-line. Clearly, a positive attitude supports student learning.

In fact, the literature review conducted by Dillon and Gabbard (1998) found substantial evidence that individual characteristics (e.g., ability, preference for active learning) do contribute to learners' success in hypermedia environments, which (given the wide variability of individuals) may explain why so many earlier studies produced conflicting results. Hartley and Bendixen (2001) also provide a rationale and evidence that self-regulatory skills (e.g., ability to set goals, monitor understanding) and epistemological beliefs (about the nature of knowledge and knowing) also affect learning success in on-line settings (see Brooks, 1997; Jacobson and Spiro, 1995). For example, individuals who believe that knowledge is the sum of simple facts will not be able to solve complex problems or thrive in nonlinear, multidimensional environments such as one finds in some on-line courses (Schommer, Crouse, and Rhodes, 1992; Jacobson and Spiro, 1995). As for self-regulation, Cennamo, Ross, and Rogers (2002) describe a Web-based course that was used to improve the self-regulation behavior of students, suggesting that even if students come to on-line learning without these skills, they can acquire them while learning on-line.

Attitude, Motivation, Preparation

A student's attitude toward and access to information technology could also affect his or her performance. It is interesting, although not surprising, to find that students vary in their acceptance of Web-based education. Hiltz (1997) and Cerny and Heines (2001) also found that all students do not immediately prefer the new medium. About 60 percent of Hiltz's students expressed interest in taking another ALN course, and many students surveyed by Cerny and Heines preferred the traditional face-to-face classroom. Terry (2001) found dropout rates were higher in on-line courses (compared with traditional courses), mostly because they were not "able to adjust to the self-paced approach." (In other studies [Sener, 2001], the dropout rate is lower.) These studies contain two important—and confounding—issues, however. First, students may be responding less to on-line learning than to the asynchronous, self-paced instructional design sometimes used in ALNs and other on-line courses. The remedy may be some sort of asynchronous synchronicity, allowing some self-paced learning with regular points that students must meet, or more proactive oversight by the instructor. For example, Miller and Corley (2001) studied the effects of positive and negative e-mails and found that a negative e-mail sent from the faculty to the student who had not been participating in on-line course modules increased the student's activity significantly (positive e-mails had no effect). Second, no one medium will be best for all students: neither the lecture nor on-line course will suit all students. This finding may be the result of different learning styles, but it is not clear whether it is because of a learning style that a student would not prefer learning via technology. One would continue to expect that a percentage of students would not perform well in on-line courses and, once identified, should be counseled away from enrolling in them.

Shaw and Pieter (2000) found students thought the use of ALNs made the material easier to understand, but the less they liked the technology (or had difficulty getting access to it), the less they contributed to discussions. Bothun (1998) found some students had difficulty transitioning to the self-directed ALN and did not complete work or took "incompletes"; others who were more motivated performed well. Mason and Weller (2001) found that students were most concerned about the time it took to learn to use the computer and Web, which is matched by a high sense of accomplishment and satisfaction when the new skills are acquired. Patience and motivation were crucial in helping overcome the usual problems of course start-up and learning new skills. And although students experience greater interaction with the teacher and greater participation in the class (Fredericksen and others, 2000b), their own motivation levels also impact satisfaction with the course and their perceived learning. This study also uncovered the importance students place on "doing something," which is more likely to occur in the on-line course than in the face-to-face course, where showing up is sufficient.

In a factor analysis of at-risk student characteristics, Osborne (2001) found that the primary variables responsible for distinguishing between completers and noncompleters of Web-based courses were having a supportive study environment, motivation, computer confidence, educational level, GPA, number of credit hours taken in the semester, and number of previous distance learning courses. These variables are consistent with existing theories of college students' attrition and retention, with the exception of prior experience with distance learning (although having prior experience generally tends to help in current circumstances, irrespective of specific characteristics of that experience). Stinson and Claus (2000) also found that students in an on-line class had lower absenteeism, fewer late assignments, and higher overall grades (and a better attitude toward taking a required course).

In a case study of students in on-line courses, Baylen and Tyler (1998) found that students' expectations and perceptions of on-line learning affected student outcomes. Student expectations that an on-line course might be easier or less structured indicated to faculty that these perceptions need to be "managed," with a clear explanation of what demands would be placed on students.

Lynch (2001) addressed the effective preparation of students for on-line learning by creating an on-line course that began with three "self-assessments": computer skills, distance education suitability, and learning style. The course asked students to research the differences of on-line learning, analyze their learning preferences, devise ways to adapt their learning style to the on-line setting, practice creating Word and html documents, and practice social communications in a chat room and role-playing situation. Almost 75 percent of the graduates of the course increased their independent, self-directed learning, 94 percent understood their learning style and could adjust their style to the on-line format, and attrition declined from 35 percent to 15 percent. This experience argues for better and more proactive preparation of students for the on-line learning environment and that such preparation can be effective.

Gender

Gender, although given substantial attention as an important determinant of younger children's computer skills, seems not to be a factor in college-level on-line learning. Ory, Bullock, and Burnaska (1997) compared attitudes toward the asynchronous learning network model and found no significant gender differences. Sullivan (1998) provides an excellent review, focusing on how on-line discussions result in equal participation of males and females, especially in contrast to how males and females communicate face to face. On-line discussions also depend on the contribution of everyone, which allows the shyer or less aggressive student to contribute at any time rather than being left out of classroom discussions where quickness and a loud voice help one get recognized. And in the on-line class, there is no "live human being in front of us sending out all sorts of 'information' about herself . . . [like] the clothes she wears, the style of her hair, the way she dresses, the color of her skin" (Sullivan, 1998). In this way, the ways we often judge other people are removed, and we are left with assessing others by the content of their contributions. For these reasons, on-line education may be a far more welcoming and equalizing environment for women (or the shy, the minority, or handicapped individual) than a more traditional classroom.

Blum (1999) discovered a different view of the role of gender. Based on content analyses of communications in ALN courses, Blum found differences in male and female messages that mirror traditional, face-to-face communications. Males were more likely to control on-line discussions, post more questions, express more certainty in their opinions, be more concrete, and provide less personal information about the speaker. Females were more empathetic, polite, and agreeing (often followed by "but"), supplied the niceties that maintain relationships (such as "please" and "thank you"), and asked questions. Females were more prone to face dispositional (lack of confidence), situational (lack of time), and institutional (lack of technical skills) barriers than their male counterparts. Although Sullivan (1998) may express the hope advocates hold for the Internet, it is likely that we will, as a society, take our prejudices and behaviors with us when we join on-line courses, as Blum (1999) discovered.

Benefits to Learning: Transfer, Critical Thinking, and Writing

Some evidence suggests that learning in an environment that allows for connections, such as a Web-based course that has many hypertext links, will improve the transfer of learning to new situations. Jacobson and Spiro (1995) compared learning that stressed simple versus multiple themes in test cases and found that students in the control condition were better at memorizing factual knowledge while those in the experimental condition, focusing on multiple themes in a hypertext environment, performed better on knowledge transfer. This study is an interesting test of cognitive flexibility theory, which may be particularly appropriate for Web-based learning.

Another useful question is whether on-line work can improve critical thinking. Newman, Webb, and Cochrane (1999) used content analysis of on-line messages to look for critical-thinking indicators in computer conferences. Students were more likely to make important statements and link ideas, although they contributed fewer novel ideas than the face-to-face comparison group. This finding may indicate that on-line conversations are less suited to operations like brainstorming, or that working on-line encourages respondents to work in a linear fashion, linking comments to earlier statements and bringing in outside knowledge. Shapley (2000) also looked at complex reasoning in chemistry courses and found the on-line students scored slightly higher, generating a similar score on an American Chemical Society exam that requires complex reasoning skills as graduate students. In another case study of on-line courses, students felt they learned to think more critically and that they could not get through the course by working hard only at exam times (Eklund and Eklund, 1996).

Garrison, Anderson, and Archer (2001) also looked at critical thinking in computer-mediated communications through a four-stage process: (1) triggering (posing the problem), (2) exploration (search for information), (3) integration (construction of possible solution), and (4) resolution (critical assessment of solution). Transcripts of on-line discussions were coded, resulting in 8 percent of the responses coded as triggers, 42 percent as exploration, 13 percent as integration, and 4 percent as resolution. The authors hypothesize that the low numbers for integration and resolution may be the result of the need for more time to reflect on the problem and that individuals would hesitate to offer inadequate solutions to avoid rejection. Garrison, Anderson, and Archer (2001) also coined the term *cognitive presence* as the "extent to which learners are able to construct and confirm meaning through sustained reflection and discourse in a critical community of inquiry" (p. 11), which is a useful concept to add to the language about on-line discussions. Clearly, they are promising areas of research, and later studies will likely extend or adjust the understandings gleaned from these studies.

Ample evidence also exists for the impact of on-line learning on writing skills. One example is Wegerif's study (1998) of ALNs, which found the ALN model to improve writing skills, largely through regular and ample opportunities to communicate via discussion boards and threaded discussions with other students. Similar studies abound, including Peha's description (1997) of using on-line debates to improve students' persuasive writing skills, Wade (1999), and Kuh and Vesper (1999), among others.

What is needed, however, is research into whether a "match" between personal qualities and technologies can demonstrably improve learning, whether use of some technologies impact (support, oppose, or change) these qualities, and how personal qualities overcome barriers to learning (see Garland, 1993).

Learning Styles

Learning styles have long been of interest to educational researchers—and no less so to researchers into Web-based education. A definition of learning styles from Sarasin (1999) includes the ability to analyze and understand learning as a result of the primary sense involved (visual, auditory, tactile, or kinesthetic), psychological aspects (e.g., cognitive, perceptual, behavioral, affective), or the method of processing information (e.g., concrete, abstract, sequential, random). Other definitions of learning styles focus on the individual's ability to learn by direction, interaction, inquiry, or creation (Whitesel, 1998), and although learners may have a preference or strength, the "effectiveness of the learning environment increases when all four styles can be accommodated." Similarly, instruction should work with the individual's strengths and strengthen his or her weaknesses (Sarasin, 1999).

Examples include research into learning styles and locus of control (Dille and Mezack, 1991; Stone, 1992), which found that concrete, external learners might have more problems with distance learning. Indications are that the ascendance of asynchronous, Web-based learning may moderate these issues, although additional research into the interaction of learning styles with the different types of technology is needed. Does Web-based instruction impact the individual's learning style? And if student learning styles change continually, changing from year to year and from the beginning to the end of term (Grasha, 1996), how might the interaction between learning styles and technology be used to change, inhibit, or encourage new learning styles, thereby helping students develop many styles for different situations?

In an assessment of students' learning and study strategies inventory (LASSI) and performance in ALNs, Loomis (2000) found significant associations with five LASSI scales: attitude, time management, concentration, selecting main ideas, and study aids. *Attitude* and *selecting main ideas* were predictors for whether the student dropped out of class, which may indicate that students with less interest in mastering the ALN environment or who were unable to see the main ideas in the rich on-line environment had the most problems. *Time management* was the strongest predictor of performance in the class, indicating that the time demands of on-line learning must be made clear to students. *Concentration* was important, given the asynchronous nature of the learning experience, indicating that students with less ability to concentrate on academic tasks may do less well in this environment. *Study aids* was important to success, because it indicated the student's ability to use and understand the multilayered design of ALN courses.

Diaz and Bontenbal (2001) found differences between on-line and traditional learners. On-line learners had higher scores on an independent learning scale and lower scores on the collaborative and dependent learning scales. After additional analysis, on-line learners were found to be willing to work in collaborative environments, but they needed structure from the instructor on how to initiate it and proceed. The authors then describe the kind of instructional tools available through the Web that address these preferences. Dziuban, Moskal, and Dziuban (2000) looked at behavior types that prefer aggressive versus passive and independent versus dependent behaviors and found that these types were evenly distributed across face-to-face courses but that aggressive-dependents and aggressive-independents were 80 percent of the students in on-line courses. In addition, dependents preferred, and independents felt less need for, face-to-face instruction.

Whether a student prefers a more visual or verbal learning style may also affect his or her learning on-line. Becker and Dwyer (1998) studied students pursuing a group project using groupware (software allowing group conversations and mutual working space). Students with a visual learning style felt that "use of groupware enhanced their group project experience and helped the project run more smoothly"; students with a verbal learning preference were less pleased in their assessments of the group's effectiveness and the group process. Florida Gulf Coast University has students complete the Myers-Briggs Type Indicator so they can be aware of how they engage the world and, by inference, learn best (Twigg, 2001a). (Readers looking for a thoughtful discussion of cognitive styles and modifications for distance education should see Liu and Ginther [1999].)

The importance of learning styles may go beyond determining and understanding how or why some styles do better with a particular instructional activity or type of technology. Twigg (2001a) has made an impassioned plea that institutions not duplicate existing courses when they go on-line but take advantage of the Web's flexibility to provide more options for students and address a variety of learning styles. In this view, "Greater quality means greater individualization of learning experiences for students" (Twigg, 2001a, p. 9). The opportunities for individualized learning may well be the hallmark of quality for future on-line learning courses.

Humanity and the Spirit

Perhaps one of the more disturbing criticisms of the use of technology is its purported impact on "the human mind, body, spirit, and community" (Healy, 1999). The assumption is that technology will make its users less human, damage the spirit, and make distance learners less capable of achieving community. Others charge that on-line communication is "disembodied," which may have serious consequences to how participants view the reality of others and the consequences of actions taken from the virtual environment to the real world. These charges are serious, and they are echoed in stories of Internet addiction and isolation. Alternately, Harasim (1995) states that "media enable us to communicate and form communities . . . [which] makes us more human" (p. 1). Which of these views of our humanity best describes the Internet, or are both only a reflection of the needs that individuals take to this new environment?

Bellcourt (1998) focuses on technology's ability to bridge space and time in a relationship rather than being limited to face-to-face conversations set in a particular time and place. Thus, electronic interaction is "not any better or worse than face-to-face interaction—it is simply different." He concludes that it can, when used wisely, enhance our humanity.

Altany (2000) argues that the best use of the new technologies will be to "transcend that very technology," to focus on learning, which is "what humans do and are and is, thus, a spiritual heritage . . . a spiritual experience." Technology is not contrary to learning and can enhance it by providing a "meditative still point" to contemplate one's perspective against the information provided and evolve it into wisdom. Similar to this idea is the solitude and "stillness" necessary to learning as one takes the time to listen deeply to others, to respond to or ask a question, and to see "one's own thoughts unfold on the monitor screen as one types." Technology with soul teaches humility, the elusiveness of cyberspace, and the strangeness of computer chips creating prose on screen. These are the conditions for technology to transform our "perception of the world and our place in it," creating connections and community and a sense of responsibility for their own and others' learning. Altany criticizes how technology is used ("a gathering and gleaning of information"), which is a view of education that bedevils the use of technology. What is perhaps most positive in this discussion, however, is the sense that technology can be used in ways that enhance one's sense of spirituality, if that is what one intends to achieve.

Quality research—however difficult to design—must be attempted to resolve some of these issues, fairly and without prejudice. Whether Internet use or on-line education has an effect on one's human characteristics may be the result of one's aims or preexisting values rather than an independent effect of using the technology. In this view, it may turn out that on-line classes are impervious to these influences because they are characterized and entered into as learning tools, yet excessive use may subtly influence how students see themselves and others. On the other hand, if we remember that most college students have had and are having numerous experiences and relationships that are face to face or normal in other ways,

Whether Internet use or on-line education has an effect on one's human characteristics may be the result of one's aims or preexisting values rather than an independent effect of using the technology.

perhaps the influence of Internet use (if there is one) will be heavily moderated by students' day-to-day lives.

Generational Differences

The more experienced and motivated learner has had, in the past, the greatest likelihood of succeeding in the distance learning environment. But what of the Gen X or Gen Y learner? Certainly, using and manipulating the technology may be easier for the younger learner, but are the learning skills and self-sufficiency there to support the learner and help him or her succeed? B. Brown (1997) reviewed the literature on ways of learning for this new generation of students and found seven trends:

1. Having grown up with both parents working, students are independent problem solvers and self-starters, and although they may want help, they resist control.
2. Because many grew up with computers, they are technologically literate.
3. They crave stimulation and expect immediate answers and feedback.
4. They are focused and do not want to waste time doing work that is not meaningful.
5. They know they must be lifelong learners to stay marketable.
6. They are ambitious and crave success on their own terms.
7. They are often fearless.

These characteristics indicate the usefulness of new teaching strategies, including a focus on constructing knowledge, doing and experiencing, and allowing the learner to control his or her experiences, which may be particularly suitable for Web-based learning experiences.

Brain research indicates that older learners (and many faculty) have laid down synapses that support text-based, linear thinking and learning and that Gen Y learners have laid down synapses that support visual, analogical connections (Healy, 1999). In other words, all their computer use in the early years may have increased the likelihood that these students' learning style is predominantly visual and that they use analogy to make sense of their environments. Healy (1999) concludes that younger brains influenced by the rapid-fire, visually stimulating new media are different in ways that faculty may not detect or understand and that many instructional models (be they for on-line courses or on-campus classrooms) do not support.

What other types of generational differences might one expect to see? Tuller and Oblinger (1999) describe a generation that will take the Internet for granted, orient differently in space and time from earlier generations, be "global, connected, and around-the-clock," and as comfortable with computers as they are with refrigerators. They ask whether higher education is ready for students with these new skills and preferences.

Self-Assessment Tools

Perhaps in response to the importance of the learner in determining success in the on-line environment, several self-assessment tools have been developed to help students assess their aptitude or likelihood of learning successfully in an on-line or distance education course. Most popular tools are on-line and can be found at institutional Web sites where distance education is offered. A review of these tests reveals their dependence on the existing research on learning styles, study habits, and other qualities and the importance of being able to be an independent learner with ample motivation. The *Distance Learner's Guide* (Western Cooperative for Educational Telecommunications, 1999) is an in-depth version of the self-assessment tool, helping the potential distant learner to find, evaluate, and choose a learning program that will be most conducive to student learning.

Summary

This chapter provides some insight into the impact of the Web on student learning. Much of the research on Web-based courses (whether comparison studies or case studies) indicates that students do as well or better and are satisfied with their learning experiences. Ample interaction (with material, students, and faculty) and constructivist learning situations (e.g., project- and problem-based learning) enabled by the Web may be the key to this improved performance. But student learning may also depend on a number of individual qualities, including a positive attitude and motivation, independence, sufficient computer skills, a predominantly visual learning style, and an understanding that learning is not a passive process of absorbing information. These individual differences make it difficult to promote any one approach as good for everyone. Intriguing evidence also exists that on-line educational environments develop critical-thinking and writing skills and improve the transfer of learning.

Yet research must begin to address several important questions. Are there differences in the effect of the Web by discipline or level of study? Are there optimal mixes of media (some combination of face-to-face and Web-based courses, for example) for student learning? Will Web-based learning have a McLuhan-type effect on those who use it? Is there an optimal match of individual student characteristics or learning styles and on-line applications? Will there be an impact on our spiritual natures or the brains of the young? These are pressing questions, yet the next chapter, on the role of faculty and institutions on developing quality on-line learning, will generate more.

Research on Faculty
and Institutions

THIS CHAPTER FOCUSES ON EVIDENCE that faculty and their institutions affect the quality of on-line learning. For faculty, the research looks at individual qualities, including age and motivation, policies (such as rewards), satisfaction (and its relationship to workload), pursuit of professional development, and knowledge about instructional design. Institutions also play a role in creating conditions for quality through their commitment to and management of on-line learning as well as their focus on learning and student outcomes assessment and their prevailing model of education. Finally, the chapter discusses the impact of on-line learning on the transformation of the institution.

The Role of Faculty

This section reviews research that focuses on the characteristics and qualities of faculty engaged in Web-based learning, and which of those qualities may best contribute to a successful experience for both students and faculty.

Faculty Qualities

With the advent of the Web, faculty will increasingly be called upon to be content experts and instructional designers, and adept at understanding pedagogy, the new technology, and learning in an on-line environment. (Gillespie [1998] provides a good review of the extent of issues affecting faculty through the introduction of technology.) Although faculty development opportunities increasingly focus on teaching faculty the how-to's of teaching on-line, what types of faculty characteristics or aptitude would indicate the potential for a successful educational experience for students? Certainly they might include interest in learning new skills, willingness to change how one does work, and comfort with communicating on-line, but they also include flexibility and a tolerance for frustration and the usual inexplicable technological glitches. Age may also be a determining factor, as younger faculty have technology skills, may expect to teach on-line, or are willing to develop their skills to do so. Schifter's study (2002) notes the way younger faculty respond differently from older faculty to certain motivators; she concludes that "concerns of junior, untenured faculty need careful consideration," especially when the demand for research is taken into consideration.

Smith, Tyler, and Benscote (2000) suggest the types of behaviors that on-line instructors should have or develop: being a team player, working well ahead of the course delivery schedule, and considering content as well as delivery mechanisms and technical support. They need to be able to adapt "fundamental communication skills that enable them to communicate, relate to and interact with students" to the on-line setting and be flexible, develop backup plans, and recognize that "even with the best of planning, things may go wrong."

In a survey of its members, the National Education Association (2000) found that 72 percent of faculty experienced with distance learning are positive about the experience, while 14 percent hold a negative opinion. Faculty teaching over the Web are more likely to be positive, rate their Web-based courses higher than their non-Web-based courses for some student learning outcomes (but not all), and believe it is unlikely that the quality of education would decline as a result of using the Web. These results suggest that perhaps experience with using the Web is the best way to turn faculty who have doubts about the medium into supporters.

Should some faculty not teach on-line, and can some faculty not translate their special strengths to the on-line environment? Would the faculty person who finds on-line communications unsatisfying do more harm than good if teaching over the Web? Would the exceptional lecturer not adapt to on-line instruction? Although there has been no research completed on these issues to date, perhaps one viable answer is to reverse the qualities of successful on-line faculty. For example, the inflexible, the easily frustrated, and the technically inept would do well to stay away, if possible. The lecturer may balk at the Web environment, and others will not be satisfied without being able to perform on the classroom stage. And certainly, some faculty see no reason to change, as they hold students responsible for their own learning irrespective of faculty choice of instructional model and technology (Cárdenas, 1998). Or it is possible that those faculty who may not be successful (or feel they may not be) have self-selected themselves out of experimenting with on-line learning. In either case, they are worthwhile questions to ask, and they are essential to prevent faculty (and their students) from having unnecessarily unpleasant experiences on-line.

Motivation and Rewards

In a factor analysis of motivators and inhibitors for teaching on-line, Schifter (2000, 2002) surveyed faculty and administrators and found four scales (in order of loading): intrinsic motives (e.g., challenge, improve teaching), personal needs (e.g., release time, monetary reward), inhibitors (e.g., lack of release time, lack of support), and extrinsic motives (e.g., requirement of department, support of administrators). For faculty, responses were also split between those who had participated in distance education and those who had not; those who had taught on-line were more likely to name intrinsic motives, while those who had not named more extrinsic motives. Administrators were more likely to name personal needs and extrinsic motivators as influencing whether faculty participate in distance learning. Fredericksen and others (2000a) had similar results, finding that faculty motivated to try on-line teaching were interested in the Internet or on-line teaching and that they rated the experience more satisfying than those whose motivation was a fear of being left behind.

Betts (1998) also looked at the motivations for involvement with distance education and found that faculty were (again) motivated by intrinsic factors (e.g., intellectual challenge) and inhibited by lack of release time and technical support; extrinsic factors (e.g., credit toward promotion, merit pay) did not affect their involvement. Deans thought the top motivating factors for faculty were money, credit toward tenure, and release time. In another study of incentives, Rockwell, Schauer, Fritz, and Marx (1999) also found that faculty were motivated by such incentives as providing innovative instruction and using new teaching techniques, that monetary awards were neither an incentive nor an obstacle, and that the biggest obstacles were time and training. These studies present a consistent picture of the intrinsic motivators that push faculty into getting involved in on-line learning and find consistently that administrators overestimate the importance of extrinsic motivations. On the other hand, these studies also seem to imply that to involve the faculty who are not motivated by the same factors may well take money, time, and rewards.

Although the emphasis on intrinsic rewards is interesting, what is more interesting is how impervious faculty have been to negative rewards (or the lack of extrinsic rewards). Wolcott (1997) found that many institutions did not reward faculty for their on-line teaching, nor were promotion and tenure decisions influenced positively by a faculty person's developing Web-based courses. This is an interesting quandary: policy discourages a behavior that some faculty pursue anyway, while other faculty avoid the activity because of the lack of extrinsic rewards. Although there are probably multiple answers to this issue, reward and tenure policies aligned to support on-line learning may encourage some of the more reluctant faculty to pursue on-line teaching. On the other hand, a favorable policy may not be sufficient to change faculty behavior; it is not necessary, but it does enable faculty involvement for those so motivated.

Advice from Other Faculty

As mentioned in Chapter Two, numerous articles discuss faculty members' sharing their experiences teaching on-line and providing advice to others. Girod and Cavanaugh (2001) share examples of how faculty can use technology to extend what is currently done (perhaps making it better) or radically change what is done and how it is done. Suggestions include moving toward a more constructivist model of learning and a learner-centric model of the classroom.

Sulla (1999) provides a worthwhile review of how using technology changes the faculty role, emphasizing the need for faculty to facilitate learning by asking connection, synthesis, and metacognition questions, and helping students identify what they need to know, what they understand, and how to apply what they know. Other examples of this type of article, which document the changes made in curricula or pedagogy, management, and relationships with students, include Stith (2000), White (2000), Coppola, Hiltz, and Rotter (2001), Dereshiwsky (2000), Hoffman (2001), and the papers of several University of Indiana faculty (see http://www.ihets.org/distance_ed/ fdpapers/1998/index.html). Their advice appears generally sound, although one cannot claim that it is always based on research. Sometimes the brave authors share advice that has been derived by suffering failure, the type of experience that teaches all of us what works and what does not.

The Impact of "Presence"

One intriguing idea is the evidence that a personal presence is important in Web-based classes. Gunawardena and Zittle (1997) found that "social presence" (the degree to which a person is perceived as real in an on-line conversation) is a strong predictor of satisfaction with computer-mediated communications. Arbaugh (2001) calls this phenomenon *immediacy behaviors,* as they reduce the "social distance" between teachers and students; in this study, these types of behaviors were positive predictors of student learning and course satisfaction.

A study by Anderson, Rourke, Garrison, and Archer (2001) also addressed the issue of presence. The authors reviewed transcripts of course discussions held over computer conferencing systems and developed the concept of *teaching presence,* expressed by comments in three categories: design and organization (e.g., "This week we will discuss . . . "), facilitating discourse (e.g., "I think we are getting off track"), and direct instruction (e.g., "Bates says . . . "). Faculty who are adept at expressing their personalities over e-mail or other Web-based communications may be at an advantage in connecting with students, which may help students then bond to the instructor or instructional experience.

Faculty Satisfaction and Workload

Although faculty satisfaction derives from many factors, in distance education it may determine whether faculty return to the on-line classroom or advocate becoming involved with on-line teaching to other faculty. In a study of faculty satisfaction in ALNs, Hartman, Dziuban, and Moskal (2000) found that faculty satisfaction and student outcomes were strongly related, indicating that most faculty are motivated and rewarded by success in student learning. Faculty in the ALNs experienced increased interaction (and improved quality of interaction) with students over traditional classrooms. Time demands to achieve this interaction were, however, "severe." Fredericksen and others (2000a), in a study of the factors influencing faculty satisfaction with asynchronous teaching in the SUNY Learning Network, found near 100 percent satisfaction with the teaching experience; 48 percent felt interaction with on-line students was higher, and 45 percent felt on-line students performed better. "Those who felt that their on-line students did better also felt significantly more satisfied with on-line teaching."

The Higher Education Research Institute (1998) surveyed faculty and found the advent of information technology to cause inordinate stress. "Keeping up with information technology" was named as a stressor by 67 percent of the faculty surveyed and was the fourth (among women) and fifth (among men) highest stressor. Stress and time spent on information technology may be related: 87 percent of faculty use e-mail, 85 percent use computers for writing, 55 percent use computers to work from home, 38 percent use information technology to create presentations, and 27 percent use it for data analysis. As for use of the Internet, 36 percent place course assignments on the Internet, and 22 percent use it for course instruction. (Not surprisingly, more young faculty than older faculty use computers.) These figures seem to imply that many faculty have already adopted a great many uses for the computer, even if only 11 percent use it for on-line discussions and 2 percent have taught a course on-line. Perhaps these latter uses will in time develop as a natural extension of the earlier uses.

These studies point to one of on-line learning's drawbacks from the point of view of faculty: the increased workload of designing and delivering a novel and more highly interactive learning experience. Data from a national survey indicate that faculty who teach a distance education class do spend more time answering e-mails from students (National Center for Education Statistics, 2002). Interviews with experienced Internet instructors led Smith, Ferguson, and Caris (2001) to remark on the long hours but also the "intellectually challenging forum [that] elicits deeper thinking on the part of the students . . . [and more] one-to-one relationships" between faculty and students. Hartman and Truman-Davis (2001) found a similar, statistically significant positive correlation between faculty satisfaction and both the amount and quality of interaction in ALN courses studied. Obviously, a positive relationship exists between interaction with students and faculty satisfaction, just as a negative relationship exists between increased interaction and perceived increases in workload. The question is whether the additional workload is deemed worthwhile, given the positive benefits of increased contact with students. Arvan and Musumeci (2000), in a series of case studies on the Sloan Center for Asynchronous Learning Environments, found both faculty satisfaction and a higher workload. The key intervening variable seems to be the faculty's perception of student learning (whether better or more than in other classes). Similarly, Jones, Lindner, Murphy, and Dooley (2002) investigated the impact of three constructs (competence with distance education, value of distance education, information technology support) on faculty perceptions of distance education. Only the faculty person's perception that distance education had value (in terms of improving instruction or providing students a better learning environment) was related to a positive philosophical position toward distance education. This finding seems to be one of the points made by Presby (2001) and is also captured by the following faculty statement: "Students ask us as faculty and administrators to do more, to learn more, to cope with more. But it has been the qualitative improvements in student learning that sustained us through more 'the system is down' crises than we'd care to remember" (Mellow, Sokenu, and Lynch-Donohue, 1998, p. 30). It looks as though the answer to whether the additional workload is worthwhile is a resounding *yes*.

It looks as though the answer to whether the additional workload is worthwhile is a resounding *yes*.

It may be, however, that the perceived increase in workload is more specific than originally thought. Visser (2000) found that Web-based courses did require more time and effort to develop and teach but concluded that the time and effort expended "may partially depend on the accumulation of instructor experience and the level of institutional support." In other words, faculty do get better at using Web-based learning, and their improvement creates time-efficiencies. DiBiase (2000) compared a traditional to a mature on-line course and found that the on-line course did not require more effort; in fact, on a per-student basis, the on-line course required less teaching and maintenance time. These studies seem to imply that faculty effort on Web-based learning will be a function of their growing expertise and the maturity of the course: faculty learning these skills for the first time or developing a new course will surely experience an increase in their workload. But time and effort will pay off as experience is gained and expertise with the medium improves.

Professional Development

Based on Rogers's work (1995) on the theory of diffusion of innovations, Geoghegan (1994) hypothesized that faculty also fall into those who are Innovators, Early Adopters, Early Majority, and Late Majority (Laggards may never adopt an innovation or be the last to do so many years later). He further hypothesized that faculty fall into two groups: those who adopt technology without support (the Innovators and Early Adopters) and those who, although supporting technology and improved student learning, are more risk averse and need help in doing so as expeditiously as possible (the Early Majority and Late Majority). The first group needed only the equipment; the second needed appropriate professional development opportunities. Hagner and Schneebeck (2001) modify Rogers somewhat and group faculty into four "waves": *entrepreneurs, risk aversives, reward seekers,* and *reluctants.* They conclude, as did Geoghegan, that providing appropriate and timely professional development is essential for the risk aversives and that revising reward policies is important for the reward seekers. As for the reluctants, they conclude that it is "neither time- nor cost-effective to attempt to incorporate philosophically resistant faculty into institutional transformation" (p. 5).

Edmonds (1999) discusses the barriers to faculty members' using technology as vision (understanding what technology can do), time and resources, knowledge about how best to teach with the technology, and training on how to teach and organize classroom functions. Training has been identified as a core learning issue for community college faculty, who note that however important training may be, it takes time in addition to current work responsibilities (Milliron and Miles, 1998). In a survey of faculty experienced with teaching graduate courses on-line, Baxter and Miller (1998) found that faculty indicated that course administration was one of the most important factors when considering quality; this finding may indicate a special need for professional development to address faculty's understanding of how Web-based courses can operate and be managed for the mutual benefit of students and faculty.

Whether training is successful may also depend on how well it modifies the faculty's "rationalized myths" (Jaffee, 1998), the belief that classroom instruction is the "single best and necessary means" for student learning. (Burbules and Callister [2000] call this romanticizing the reality of the classroom, which for students may be dull, boring, and frustrating.) These myths are powerful not because there is empirical evidence to support them but because of "deep-seated consensual beliefs and long-standing tradition." Jaffee (1998) further hypothesizes that resistance to change results from reinforcement of the individual's identity by organizational practices. This relationship may explain the significant resistance many faculty have to on-line learning, as it violates their identity as a professor and expert, a source of knowledge and information, and a performer at the classroom lectern. Pressures to change this identity may meet substantial resistance, although changes in organizational practice and the introduction of younger faculty who do not identify with this role will likely erode this resistance. In other words, training may be important, but it may not have the impact with all faculty that some would hope.

Jaffee's point (1998) that faculty self-perception may impede the development of on-line learning may be the reason so many faculty look longingly to the time when there will be sufficient bandwidth in networks to allow for streaming video as a way to deliver their courses. In other words, they may long for the same experience (for them) of a class: to lecture and to perform and to be seen as the expert. When videos of faculty teaching were compared with audio without video, however, Wisher and Curnow (1999) found that student learning did not improve with the video capability. Video, then, may be more essential for faculty to perceive effectiveness than having an independent role in improving learning.

Rethinking as a Path to Quality?

When faculty take an existing course that began as a face-to-face course, the challenge of developing it as an on-line course forces them to "confront and analyze the material in new and different ways" (Smith, Ferguson, and Caris, 2001). Gilbert and Green (1995) found a similar result, noting that faculty increasingly reported an improvement in the quality and effectiveness of their teaching as a result of using some form of information technology.

In this view, something inherent in contemplating use of the Web encourages faculty to ask basic questions about what is intended and why and how it may be accomplished. Buchanan (1999) proposes a list of eleven questions to ask of prospective on-line teachers, including (1) What is your teaching philosophy? (2) What is the most important part of your pedagogy? (3) Are you comfortable listening to your students' perspectives and opinions? (4) Are you able to condense multiple perspectives into a coherent discussion? By facing a new medium, faculty may instigate a search for assistance, bringing them to professional development opportunities, or it may simply be the prod to rethink the activities and beliefs that one has held for so many years. The inadvertent value of the growing use of the Web may be its ability to encourage faculty to question their unquestioned beliefs, reevaluate their standard approaches, learn new skills, and rethink their classes.

> **The inadvertent value of the growing use of the Web may be its ability to encourage faculty to question their unquestioned beliefs, reevaluate their standard approaches, learn new skills, and rethink their classes.**

Instructional Design

What may occur when faculty are faced with using the Web in instruction is the need to, perhaps for the first time, understand and better use instructional design elements. In a survey of on-line instructors, Berge (1997) found the main characteristics of on-line teaching to be student-centered, self-reflective, collaborative, and authentic learning, or a rejection of more teacher-centered models (it is not clear whether more student-centered teachers are drawn to on-line education or whether on-line courses change the instructors' points of view). Being student-centered and collaborative are not, one might note, characteristics of technology but qualities of the model of learning.

What is most frustrating about so many research studies reviewed is the confounding of technology with how it is used. Smith and Dillon (1999) call it the "media/method confound" or an inability to separate technology from the way it is used in instruction. So many articles describe the technology used but not the pedagogical rationales behind what was actually done using the technology. This is an important criticism of the current wave of studies, one that helps put the confusion of "no significant differences" into perspective. How could one expect differences in outcome when the same instructional design (e.g., lecture, question-and-answer) is used in both technology-based and traditional courses?

This position is akin to the one of Clark (1994), who argued that it was the instructional design that affected learning, not the technology. Taking a different view, Kozma (1994b) states that Clark's "separation of media from method creates an unnecessary and undesirable schism" (p. 16). Media and instructional approaches are essentially integrated, and method must therefore be confounded with medium. Kozma (1994a) states that "both medium and methods influence learning and they frequently do it by influencing each other" (p. 11)—which begs the question of whether the impact of each partner in this so-called integration can be separately estimated. Clearly, we need research that attempts to find ways to separate the impact of instructional design from the technology chosen to deliver the instruction, for it may be the only type of research that will answer the technology critics' worst fears.

The Role of Institutions

This section reviews research that focuses on the characteristics of institutions already engaged in Web-based learning, and which characteristics may improve the likelihood of success for students.

Commitment

The role of the institution in the adoption and use of on-line education can be characterized as enabling—or not. Especially for distance education, an institution that is equivocal in its support of Web-based learning may be unaware of how its more traditional policies (e.g., requiring student residency on campus, transfer of credit) can be barriers to students' earning a degree. Henderikx (1992) emphasized the importance of having high-level commitment to distance education, in part because of the demands it makes on resources and staff but also because it demands change in policy and practices; moreover, completing the appropriate changes will be difficult without consistent, visible, and high-level commitment.

Institutions that undertake distance education should also have a clear understanding of its role in fulfilling the institution's mission; the institution should evaluate whether it can make the substantial commitment necessary in terms of the administrative requirements Moore and Kearsley (1996) find are essential to a quality program, i.e., planning, staffing, budgeting, and quality review. Faculty may also feel the lack of support while trying to locate appropriate resources or applying for tenure or promotion. Staff may not feel the need to revise how services to distant students (e.g., registration, advising) are provided, continuing to require that students come to campus at times convenient to the institution, not the learner. These factors will affect the institution's ability to attract and retain students, although student learning may not be directly affected.

Edmonds (1999), quoting Kotter (1996), identified four barriers to an institution's successful implementation of distance education: (1) a lack of skills or knowledge, (2) formal organizational structures that make it difficult for change to occur or be sustained, (3) personnel and information systems that make it difficult to act (e.g., individuals do not want to change or change is actively resisted), and (4) implementation of change that is discouraged or blocked. These barriers provide a framework for institutions to seriously evaluate themselves—their systems, values, and policies as well as their members' openness to change—and assess whether on-line distance education can succeed or whether action must be taken to eliminate barriers to prevent its failure or slow adoption. Muilenburg and Berge (2001) also conducted a large-scale factor analysis to identify barriers to distance education; administrative structure and organizational change, faculty compensation, and student support services all pointed to an institution's readiness to make the changes necessary to make distance education a success. A third survey of on-line teachers (Berge 1998) identified sixty-nine barriers, including academic (e.g., academic calendar, course transferability), technical (e.g., lack of reliable systems, lack of connectivity), and—the most frequently mentioned barrier—cultural (e.g., resistance to change, lack of understanding what works in distance learning). Moore (1998) has distinguished poor-quality programs from high-quality programs based on a number of factors, including the lack of administrative support (to include training and design assistance) and an unwillingness to specialize, continuing to be "all things to all people." Educause (2001) has developed a Web-based decision tool or "readiness topology" to help institutions assess their readiness for engaging in on-line learning and ways to improve readiness.

Clearly, each institution needs to understand where on-line distance education fits in its vision of the institution's future and in its mission. If it is adopted, institutional leaders need to send consistent, strong messages to institutional members—faculty, staff, and students—that it values on-line learning and that it supports distance education with actions (including resources) as well as words. It is important that when leadership changes, on-line distance education remain a part of the institution's mission, or its detractors may take the opportunity to remove its resources or slow the transition to use of the Internet in instruction. For when the institution hesitates in its support of on-line education, students may be the first ones to suffer. On the other hand, as growing enrollments indicate, it is students who are most supportive of on-line distance education, which institutions would do well to understand.

A word about security is warranted, however. To ensure the security of testing, many distance programs continue to use proctored exams, hiring a reputable local person to oversee the test taking of distant students and ensuring they are who they say they are. For those who worry about these matters, Smith, Ferguson, and Caris (2001) found the "whole worry of on-line cheating a moot point. Often stronger one-on-one relationships . . . are formed in on-line courses than in face-to-face classes." Although initially an on-line class began with students seeming anonymous and without identity, personalities and concerns emerged in the written communication of threaded discussions, e-mails, and papers. In one instance where the instructor had forgotten to put the students' names on papers, he was able to match each paper with the person who wrote it.

Quality and Managing the Process

Several writers have ideas as to how to define and assess quality distance education at the institutional level. Neal (1998) speaks of the importance of discovering, defining, and fulfilling a unique mission, be that a mission for the university as a whole or of a distance education unit. This situation might argue for a specific, tailored mission statement for Web-based distance education, one that emphasizes the particular nature of the students to be served (e.g., disenfranchised, adult workers), elements of quality to be present in all courses, measures to assess student learning, and mechanisms to link information so that improvement is possible.

The development of good on-line courses requires the expertise of a number of individuals, leading many institutions to form teams to help develop on-line courses (Diaz, 2001; Tait, 1993; Taylor, 1994). This approach depends on the content expertise of the faculty person or group of faculty who can provide breadth and depth to the course. It depends on the skills of instructional designers expert in student learning and media specialists expert in using the technology to prepare appropriate visual and interactive exercises. Among them must be individuals who understand the many ways the Web or the institution's courseware package can be used.

An interesting question is whether the structure or responsibility for distance education has an impact on the growth or quality of on-line distance learning. Stone, Showalter, Orig, and Grover (2001) attempted to assess whether a centralized or decentralized organization responsible for distance education impacted the growth of courses or enrollments or student outcomes (e.g., GPA, course completion). Of all the disciplines included in the study (English/humanities, liberal arts, business, math/science, general education), only business courses were negatively impacted by institutions having a centralized distance education office. There were no impacts on the other outcome variables. If this result were to hold up after further research, it may spell good news for institutions grappling with how to organize their distance education effort. In other words, the institution can opt for a centralized approach or a decentralized one depending on its particular campus culture, the abilities of its staff, its size, and its interest in developing and offering an extensive or more modest number of on-line courses.

When managing the initiation of the use of learning technologies, Perrin (2000) argues for a phased approach, from experimentation to integration to optimization. Doing so would allow for planning to be revised, corrections pursued, and attention paid to the best timing for instituting change. Hohn (1998) has a particularly helpful overview of the organizational change process; institutions may also find other guides for managing change helpful, whether from the corporate business or educational world.

Last, higher education institutions may need to evaluate different emerging organizational models, from extending the traditional university to for-profit centers or corporate universities or even competency-based institutions. Hanna (1998) and Wolf and Johnstone (1999) have described these new organizational entities well, although it is important to note that new organizational models may develop over time and others may drop in popularity or effectiveness. In terms of organizational options, higher education may see more variety rather than less.

It is not clear, however, what the relationship of organizational model, change management strategies, or internal barriers is to the quality of on-line distance education. It is logical that perhaps the institution impacts quality of student learning in its support of faculty or in its overall commitment to quality educational experiences. It is a fruitful area for future research, one that might be able to tell us which institutional factors are most important or whether quality learning can occur despite the institution's lack of support of on-line distance education.

The Learning Revolution
With the Web comes the ability to offer an education tailored to the individual. Rather than duplicating earlier models built on the one-to-many transmission model, the Web environment can be designed to be sufficiently rich that students can pursue their own interests in a flexible fashion that allows them to construct meaning that is useful for them. The Web also enables a variety of interactions between and among faculty and students, allowing for

groups to undertake projects together, researching and evaluating information, constructing meaning together, and portraying their understandings on the Web so that it can be shared with others. The Web has the capability—if faculty use it—to transform the current paradigm for higher education and make it more learner-centered.

Although the research into effective teaching continues to grow, what can the evolving research into learning indicate about Web-based distance education? For example, when the focus is on learning rather than teaching, does the technology support or hinder that focus? When students have "control" over their learning, will they do well in a distance learning context? If the "classroom" is no longer a physical space but is in cyberspace, what is the impact on student learning?

Student Outcomes Assessment

The use of student outcomes assessment is mentioned here for its impact on evaluating and understanding whether and how well learning has occurred. If learning is the most important outcome of any educational experience, then it is the ultimate yardstick against which to evaluate on-line learning in distance education or on-campus courses. Thus, the tools of assessment are crucial to the design and implementation of evaluations of on-line learning, if learning is to be the final determinant of what quality is in the on-line experience.

Several authors have provided useful discussions of methods for assessing on-line learning. Morley (2000) gives examples of synchronous and asynchronous assessment methods and those that can assess cognitive, affective, and psychomotor skills at a distance. The Educational Resources Information Center (2001) provides an extensive overview of the types of on-line assessment, their advantages, disadvantages (including security concerns), and solutions, and the importance of continuous, interactive assessment. Morgan and O'Reilly (1999) not only discuss issues related to assessing open and distance learners but also describe ways of using technology to conduct legitimate learning assessments. Wade (1999) includes evaluation of students' responses in threaded discussions and e-mails for quality and clarity of writing and content of ideas expressed.

Two problems arise, however, when relying on learning outcomes: first, it is difficult to quantify or reliably express what learning is desired, and second, the assessment methods chosen tend to shape what is being assessed (Farber, 1998). Farber's contention (1998) that distance learning, with its focus on competencies rather than education (which is not altogether true), will divide society into those who have a traditional "education" and those with "mere" competencies must be evaluated.

Despite these concerns, the assessment literature is gradually documenting that faculty can and do create useful statements of learning that can be assessed in quantitative or qualitative fashion (or both). A review of the assessment literature is helpful in both allaying Farber's legitimate fears and understanding the issues involved. And whether distance education is more or less concerned with competencies than other types of delivery models is also debatable; it may be that the association of competencies with distance education is the result of two independent trends in higher education occurring at the same time and therefore assumed to be correlated. On the other hand, introducing new technologies (indeed, perhaps any radically new teaching or learning method) does tend to focus its novice users on basic questions about what they are trying to accomplish (e.g., learning goals) and how it may be used to achieve these ends. It may be less a characteristic of the technology (or distance education) than a human being's need to return to basic instrumental questions when it perceives that it can no longer continue doing things the same way as before.

Conceptual Model of Education

Perhaps implicit in the earlier discussions on the learning revolution and the growing importance of student outcomes assessment is a more complex model of higher education. The belief that education is mere information—or the transfer of information from one mind to another—is not only a disservice to the field but also inaccurate. To some extent, it is this view of higher education that many critics respond to, as in Talbott's tirade (1999) against "fact-shoveling" and the view of education as transfer of information "from one database or brain to another." As J. Brown and Duguid (2000) among others have noted, education is not mere information transfer, and those who suggest it is are either misguided or a greater danger to the health of education than previously thought. For if education is mere information transfer, then the instructivist model is correct, learning remains passive, and proof of learning is a regurgitation of information bits. If education—and especially higher education—is more than information, then the Web could never replace faculty, although faculty may find themselves providing a different, and perhaps more challenging, role to students.

Privateer (1999) makes the point that information technology—by providing an improved means to relay and retain information reliably and indefinitely—has an immediate and effective role in information transfer. By taking on this function, information technology could help higher education understand and explain to others what business it is in: educating the higher, intellectual faculties in individuals who can help solve society's critical problems. Privateer (1999) also notes that the true worth of information technology may be in helping faculty design and manage the sort of learning environments that produce higher levels of learning.

It is important to make clear a second point about using the Web in higher education. Some individuals (unfortunately including a few legislators) presume that one can become educated by surfing the Web for information. But this perception belies not only a misperception of what education is but also a misunderstanding of how difficult it is to find quality information on the Web. Van Dusen (2000) has provided an excellent critique of the quality of information available over the Web, which contains a "panoply of information." The Web provides access to "peer-reviewed articles, book reviews, digitized monographs, and a rapidly expanding base of electronic journals" (Van Dusen, 2000, p. 66) as well as marketing for commercial enterprises, sites promoting all sorts of personal agendas, and opportunities to pursue unsavory activities. This characteristic of the Web should not preclude using it to deliver courses or to augment courses with Web-based materials. This last point is especially important: faculty need to take greater control over the use of the Web in courses, including reviewing sites, helping students to understand and evaluate the reliability of information on different sites, and providing connections to sites that are especially pertinent to course content.

The Transformation Agenda

Many writers about higher education support the application of information technology because of its effect on higher education. Tuller and Oblinger (1999) boldly claim, "Technology is a transformation agent." Transformation occurs through a variety of means, including the disaggregation of services and unbundling instruction (Twigg and Heterick, 1997), greater productivity (Massy and Zemsky, 1995), and better responses to market forces. Works focusing on the role technology plays in transforming higher education are increasing in number and specificity, including Barone and Hagner (2001) and other publications produced by Educause.

Not surprisingly, such transformation is not desired by all. For the American Federation of Teachers (2001), it is the emphasis on the student as consumer that is worrisome, which assumes that treating the student as a consumer automatically requires that institutions please the student rather than provide the challenging and rigorous curricula that will meet "the student's long-term interests" (p. 4). Another worry is that technology will drive the way teaching is conducted, which may occur or may reflect a lack of understanding of the flexibility of the Web and the many choices faculty have when they implement an on-line course. In any case, there has been little research evidence so far that greater market competition or increasing access has had or will affect the quality of on-line learning or that a consumer focus necessarily diminishes the level of quality in an on-line course.

The critics of technology, however, justifiably point to the lack of impact on education played by such earlier technologies as radio and television. Yet Moore (1997) asserts that in those "revolutions," educators did not rise to the challenge of developing quality programs for these media. One might guess that current educators' response to the Web is different from what it was for these earlier technologies and that the time and resources currently devoted to Web-based learning might imply that the transformational aspects of the Web may become real. But a cautionary tale might be in order, as too much hype tends to bring the skeptic out in everyone.

The question remains whether the hype for transforming higher education has affected on-line learning, or the reverse. Clearly, institutions are changing and distance education is growing, but are they related and how? This area is another fruitful one for research, one that will be difficult because of the need to unravel the influence of the same external forces (e.g., legislative actions) and similar economic forces (e.g., the cost of telecommunications networks) that likely impact both distance education and the transformation of higher education.

There are, perhaps, some interesting clues in the thinking of Margaret Wheatley, in an interview by Katz (1997): "Networking is an incredibly revolutionary act. It's probably the best way to bring down an existing structure. People find each other. They find who they need. They enjoy the freedom and the creativity that's available. . . . It changes them. It changes their work. Ultimately, they're ignoring the existing structures. . . . Networking people is not a neutral act. It's a subversive activity" (p. 18). Although these remarks seem to apply to members of the "structure" (e.g., faculty and staff), they also apply to students who find each other and are changed by the encounter. In this view, the connections provided by technology and on-line learning may indeed transform learning and the structures that support learning, leading to very different organizations in the future. It is perhaps this interactive quality of the Web that contributes to G. Brown's vision (2000) of the Web as a "transformative learning technology."

Summary

We now have a view of which faculty are best suited to on-line learning and how they can ensure a better learning experience for students. They need to love learning new things, tolerate frustration, and be willing to experiment; they are likely to be positive about this new approach to teaching and return to the on-line environment again and again. They are intrinsically motivated and largely impervious to negative external rewards or inhibiting policies; they recognize the increased workload involved in preparing for and conducting on-line classes, but their satisfaction (despite the work) is tied to seeing students learn in the new environment. Professional development opportunities may need to be tailored to faculty personality type (i.e., Innovators versus Early or Late Majority) and include a greater appreciation for instructional design.

Institutions need to be clear and consistent in their commitment to on-line learning, given its demands on resources and its ability to question long-held assumptions and change the status quo. Fortunately, a variety of good approaches or models are available for managing the on-line learning program, so it is best to choose one that is consistent with the institution's primary values. Finally, on-line learning shows a strong coincidence with a renewed focus on student learning and outcomes assessment. In any case, it may also be advisable for institutions to understand their prevailing model of education—whether information transfer or the pursuit of knowledge—and how it wishes to transform itself for a different future.

Important questions remain unanswered. What are the steps by which faculty (especially the more averse to the experience) learn to succeed on-line? For whom (or when) are faculty influenced by reward structures or policies? How should professional development be tailored to different types of faculty? Should some institutions not pursue on-line learning? Can on-line learning exist without an emphasis on student learning, assessment, or the transformation of an institution?

The next chapter turns to the various sets of guidelines that draw on research on on-line education, and subsequent chapters proceed to a discussion of what definitions of quality might be most useful to institutions, faculty, and students.

The Pursuit of Guidelines

THIS CHAPTER DISCUSSES THE DEVELOPMENT of guidelines intended to shepherd the production and offering of on-line learning and distance education and their research base. It briefly discusses different guidelines or benchmarks prepared by a number of organizations and then continues with an overview of the current state of accreditation, a comparison of the various guidelines, special guides for faculty and students, and a final caution about the use of guidelines.

Using the Research You Have

In the early years when little solid, reliable research was available, practitioners pursued the development and adoption of "best practices" or guidelines to shape distance education programs and services. The first were developed in 1995 by the Western Cooperative for Educational Telecommunications (WCET) and were known as *Principles of Good Practice for Electronically Offered Academic Degree and Certificate Programs.* Principles were developed in seven areas: curriculum and instruction, role and mission, faculty support, resources for learning, student services, commitment to support, and evaluation and assessment. Numerous other guidelines have been created, some taken and modified from the WCET principles, others developed independently and then adopted by appropriate bodies. The following discussion describes these later guidelines.

As a result of a grant-funded project called Innovations in Distance Education, Penn State, Lincoln, and Cheyney Universities developed guiding principles for distance education in five categories: learning goals and content presentation, interactions, assessment and measurement, instructional media and tools, and learner support systems (Ragan, 1999).

Chickering and Ehrmann (1996) wrote that technology is a "lever" for implementing the seven principles of good practice (Chickering and Gamson, 1987) and provided numerous examples where uses of technology could support the principles. According to the seven principles, good practice:

1. encourages contacts between students and faculty;
2. develops reciprocity and cooperation among students;
3. uses active learning techniques;
4. gives prompt feedback;
5. emphasizes time on task;
6. communicates high expectations; and
7. respects diverse talents and ways of learning.

Additional guidance in applying the seven principles to evaluating on-line courses can be found in Graham and others (2001).

In 1998, the Instructional Telecommunications Council (ITC) published the following characteristics of successful distance learning programs: (1) commitment and financial support from key administrators; (2) a strong rationale for using distance learning to extend the scope of the institution; (3) a clear definition of the audience served; (4) support for faculty training and development; (5) student support services with easy student access to the institution; and (6) adequate staffing and support personnel (Gross, Gross, and Pirkl, 1998, p. 14).

In 2000, ITC published its own summary of practices regarded as standards (Tulloch and Sneed, 2000). The items fall into five categories: (1) learning goals, content presentation, and learning activities, (2) interactions, (3) assessment/measurement, (4) tools and media, and (5) faculty and faculty support. Tulloch and Sneed (2000) offer an important caution about all these best practices: "there is a danger that best practices will become treated as rules, effectively blocking innovation and change" (p. 9). They also caution that using standards for traditional instruction has led to the "use of technology to

mimic the techniques of face-to-face instruction" (p. 9). Based on this obser-
vation, one would expect that these guidelines should be different from those
for on-campus instruction, a difference that is not always obvious (except for
the statements about media).

Also in 2000, the Institute for Higher Education Policy published *Quality on the Line,* its own work on benchmarks for Internet-based distance education and an evaluation of those benchmarks by faculty, administrators, and
students at six institutions experienced with on-line education. The benchmarks that were determined *not* to be essential were in institutional support
(faculty receive incentives to develop courses, institutions reward effective
teaching); course development (student learning styles are considered, student learning styles are assessed and determine the type of course delivery,
consistency in course structure, team development of courses, course approval
by broad peer review); teaching/learning (group work required, materials promote collaboration, courses designed as modules of varying length); course
structure (expectation of minimum time per week for study, faculty
grade and return all assignments in a certain time period). Although these
benchmarks were eliminated, it is important to note that many of them
have been supported by the research literature reviewed in Chapters Four and
Five but may be very time-consuming or resource-intensive for an uncertain
reward.

Although some of the original forty-five benchmarks were deemed not to
be essential to quality student learning, three new benchmarks were added:
(1) a fail-safe technology delivery system, (2) faculty and students' agreement
on student assignments and faculty response, and (3) quick and accurate
answers to questions of student service personnel. The final set of benchmarks
are in seven areas: institutional support, course development, teaching/learn-
ing, course structure, student support, faculty support, and evaluation and
assessment. The National Education Association subsequently adopted the
final set of twenty-four benchmarks.

The American Council on Education (2001) has not developed its own
set of guidelines but has discussed the guidelines from WCET, the Council
for Higher Education Accreditation (CHEA), and NEA. Its main contribution may be a discussion of the various barriers to distributed education,

including policies (articulation, copyright, intellectual property), politics (expecting results too soon), and process (dealing with critics).

In the United Kingdom, the Quality Assurance Agency for Higher Education (2000) has published its own guidelines. The guidelines cover design, establishing academic and delivery standards, student development and support, student communication and representation, and student assessment. The Open University in the United Kingdom (Tait, 1993) has extensive quality assurance activities that involve teams of individuals creating, testing, and evaluating course materials, monitoring teaching and the time taken by tutors to respond to student assignments, and collecting feedback from students. Canada is also developing quality guidelines for on-line learning (see Barker [2001] for more information).

More Traditional Views

Placing the following sets of guidelines or best practices in a separate section is not meant to imply that they are substantially different from the guidelines of other bodies already discussed. But they are interesting for some of the conclusions drawn about quality assurance for distance education, which belie their more traditional values.

CHEA has also undertaken a review of quality assurance of distance education on behalf of the needs of accreditation entities. In a review of quality assurance strategies in distance learning, Phipps, Wellman, and Merisotis (1998) found that distance learning programs focused on faculty credentials, selection, and training; time-on-task measures; student support services and consumer information; and goals and outcomes. Although these measures are not markedly different from quality assurance measures in conventional education, Phipps, Wellman, and Merisotis (1998) remarked on the striking difference in the process of quality review, a process that did not depend on a "consensus-oriented faculty committee" but was "less consultative and more assessment-driven" (p. 23). They charge that the narrow focus on program goals and objectives "suggests a greater market orientation" (p. 23). These interpretations (and the negative judgments implied) are interesting, given that distance education tends to view at least some of these changes (i.e., clarity of program goals and objectives) as a good thing. (And there is no reason to suspect that quality in distance learning is not just as dependent on the specification and agreements of faculty.) The authors also found differences in quality assurance strategies in institutions' mission (more emphasis on teaching/learning), greater focus on client (i.e., the student), less control of faculty over curriculum (use of prepackaged courses or part-time faculty), less emphasis on process (and more assessment-driven), and contracting for services. Reading such a list one can see that Schweiger (1996) was correct: applying the criteria of traditional quality assurance measures would force distance education to duplicate the structures and processes of traditional education. Distance education was designed, however, to change these very elements in an attempt to improve on the original.

CHEA (2000), in collaboration with the National Center for Higher Education Management Systems, developed an alternative approach to accreditation standards. *Competency standards* include providing evidence of institutional accomplishments in three areas: student outcomes and attainment, responsiveness to students, and organizational alignment and support.

The American Federation of Teachers published its guidelines for good practice in 2000 based on survey results of 200 members who taught distance education courses. The standards largely focus on distance education courses (in contrast to accreditation, which focuses on programs and institutions) and include standards on granting college credit, the appropriate faculty to teach courses (and the appropriate supports for those faculty), course requirements, and technical support, among others. These standards include some requirements that continue to belie a belief that more traditional education is superior, such as "no one is offered distance education as his or her only option for obtaining an education," which ignores the conditions of many students in rural areas or with heavy family and work demands (precisely those conditions that distance education is most suited for). The AFT also, however, encourages institutions to experiment with offering a variety of subjects through distance education and become "laboratories of program evaluation," which places the responsibility for creating new approaches on the institutions best suited to implement and evaluate them. The AFT (2001) also worries about the impact of these changes on faculty prerogatives, including workload and role, as well as the emphasis on standardizing the curriculum and relying too heavily on competencies. A survey by NEA (2000) yields similar results: respondents worry about traditional union issues like workload and pay, although faculty experienced with distance education also tended to rate their Web-based courses better than their traditional courses on a number of goals (but not all). In any case, it appears that the attitude an organization takes toward on-line learning depends on the beliefs or perquisites of its main constituents.

The Latest Thinking in Accrediting Distance Education

Eaton (2001) discusses the following responsibilities of the accrediting community when it comes to assuring the quality of distance education:

1. Identify the distinctive features of distance learning delivery, whether within traditional settings or supplied by one of the new providers.
2. Modify accreditation guidelines, policy, or standards to assure quality within the distinctive environment of distance delivery.
3. Pay additional attention to student achievement and learning outcomes in the context of distance learning.
4. Work with government to adjust current policy.
5. Assume more responsibility for addressing public interest in the quality of higher education as distance learning opportunities and providers diversify and expand (Eaton, 2001, p. 11).

By the end of 2001, the eight regional accrediting associations had prepared a set of guidelines for reviewing distance education programs. The Council of Regional Accrediting Commissions (CRAC) developed best practices for evaluating evidence in five areas of interest (2001): institutional context and commitment, curriculum and instruction, faculty support, student support, and evaluation and assessment. For example, in response to criterion 2e—"The importance of appropriate interaction (synchronous and asynchronous) between instructor and students and among students is reflected in the design of the program and its courses. . . ."—several questions are posed, such as "What provisions for instructor-student and student-student interaction are included in the program/course design and the course syllabus? How is appropriate interaction assured?" The document is a guide to reviewers from the accrediting team to identify and elucidate evidence that the criteria associated with quality are present in the program and institution.

Comparing the Guidelines

Table 1 provides a high-level comparison of the five sets of major guidelines (WCET, CHEA, NEA, ITC, and CRAC) as well as Chickering and Gamson's seven principles (1987). Readers wishing more detail can follow up with the particular set of guidelines that interests them. Compiling all of the guidelines in this fashion resulted in sixty-five different standards or practices after eliminating those that are the same across the guidelines. Although the categories help in the analysis, much important detail is lost. The purpose of this analysis is not to claim or imply that one set of guidelines is better or more complete than another: all have value.

The table does make two important points about the guidelines, however. First, based on the interests of the group promoting a set of guidelines, the number of guidelines, standards, or benchmarks is greater in areas where the members might have additional interest and greater expertise. Therefore, it is not surprising to see that CHEA has more standards focusing on the assessment of student learning, NEA has the greatest number of standards concerning the teaching and learning process, and ITC has its greatest number of standards for facilities and technology.

Second, each set of guidelines has some good standards not found in other guidelines. In other words, if you or your institution needs a good set of guidelines, the best choice may be a combination of these standards, choosing and selecting those standards that fit the institution's needs and discarding those that may be of less importance.

TABLE 1
Comparison of Current Guidelines:
Number of Standards by Category

Category	WCET	CHEA	NEA	ITC	CRAC	Seven Principles
Evaluation and assessment; student outcomes	3	11	3	0	6	0
Curriculum and instruction; responsiveness to students; student learning; course development and faculty support	7	13	13	2	9	7
Student services; library and learning resources	5	1	55	1	4	—
Facilities, finances, and organizational alignment; institutional support or commitment	2	6	3	7	10	—

SOURCES: WCET: Western Cooperative for Educational Telecommunications, 1995; CHEA: Phipps, Wellman, and Merisotis, 1998; NEA: Institute for Higher Education Policy, 2000; ITC: Gross, Gross, and Pirkl, 1998; CRAC: Council of Regional Accrediting Commissions, 2000; Seven Principles: Chickering and Gamson, 1987.

Faculty Tips and Guidelines

Faculty have also prepared a number of articles about guidelines for others to better ensure a positive experience with distance learning for both the program and students. Short (2000) emphasizes hardware and computer skills, Shell (1994a, 1994b) focuses on activities for faculty (e.g., don't lecture, teach netiquette), Lefoe and Corderoy (1998) provide recommendations on structure (e.g., identify the audience and learning outcomes), Garrison and Onken (1998) focus on the sort of do's and don'ts oriented to making the first teaching experience better for faculty (e.g., "DO pretest, test and retest course materials").

The League for Innovation in the Community College published a "handbook for instructors" (Boaz and others, 1999), which provides useful guidance on designing distance learning courses, technology models, communication and collaboration, student guidance, testing and assessment, and the asynchronous community college from experienced providers. Also in 1999, the league published a guide for faculty on moving teaching and learning to the Web (Boettcher and Conrad, 1999). The guide focuses on information essential to faculty as they research the differences of Web-based education, uses of technology, good teaching and student learning practices, necessary resources, design guidelines, steps in developing Web courses, course models, creating and sustaining on-line communities, and related issues in Web-based education.

As a guide for faculty in their design of on-line courses, Alley and Jansak (2001) have developed *Ten Keys to Quality Assurance* for on-line learning that is focused on the views, values, and needs of the course consumer, whether that person is a student, instructor, or institutional officer:

1. Knowledge is constructed.
2. Learning is more effective if a student can take responsibility for her own learning.
3. Student motivation is a strong determinant of the outcomes and success of learning.
4. Higher-order learning requires reflection.
5. Learning is unique to the individual.
6. Learning is experiential.
7. Learning is both social and private.
8. Inexorable epistemological presumptions can misdirect higher-order thinking.
9. Learning is spiral.
10. Learning is "messy."

This excellent review of current learning science can be useful for faculty in their design and management of on-line courses.

Guidelines for Students

As mentioned earlier, students have available a growing number of guides for assessing their own suitability for learning on-line and evaluating courses and programs. WCET's *Distance Learner's Guide* (1999) can help the potential distance learner find, evaluate, and choose a program that will be most conducive to student learning. Other consumer guides, such as those prepared by the private college associations of Illinois, Iowa, Minnesota, and Wisconsin (see, e.g., Iowa Association of Independent Colleges and Universities, 1997), Abernathy (1999), and Strong and Harmon (1997) focus on questions that a student should consider about the institution (What are the dropout and completion rates for students?) and the course (Will the credits earned be transferable?).

Other guides to distance learning programs have rapidly become available in book and Web form, including such standards as *Peterson's Guide to Distance Learning* (a searchable version is available at http://www.petersons.com/dlearn), *Barron's Guide to Distance Learning* (http://www.barronseduc.com/), *Bear's Guide to Earning Degrees Nontraditionally* (http://www.degree.net), *LifeLong-Learning On-Line Database of Distance Learning Courses* (http://www.lifelonglearning.com), and the Princeton Review's *Best Distance Learning Graduate Programs* (http://www.geteducated.com). Given the growth of the Web and the distance learning marketplace (and services designed to help students wend their way through all the resources available), this list of guides may be incomplete. Some Web sites allow students to search for programs by discipline or type (e.g., business, bachelor's). Additional guides (see Carr, 2000) are filling bookshelves, and Web sites offering information about distance education continue to grow. In light of the importance of fair disclosure, however, students need to know how programs were selected for inclusion in the guide and whether the institution paid any remuneration to the publisher or Web site developer, as is sometimes the case.

Another source of information for students is the growing number of Web sites listing the courses or programs institutions offer via distance education, such as the Southern Regional Electronic Campus (http://www.srec.sreb.org) and Western Governors University (http://www.wgu.edu), plus the Web sites of state consortia and individual institutional sites too numerous to list (although one would not go too wrong by assuming that most states and institutions have such a site). All these sites offer some sort of search mechanism, most frequently (although not exclusively) searching on discipline or level of course as well as other criteria. Hundreds of courses can be listed on these sites, which students can search to find what they need, although questions of whether courses will be transferable or accepted by the student's institution may not be addressed.

Growing Acceptance and Criticism

Since the development of WCET's *Principles of Good Practice* (1995), each major regional accrediting association reviewed and adopted some version of the principles before creating the guidelines discussed earlier (Council of Regional Accrediting Commissions, 2000). Other accreditors that have modified and adopted these principles include the National Association of State Approving Agencies and several discipline-based accrediting associations. In addition, numerous institutions and systems have adopted WCET's principles as a way to guide development and evaluation of distance education programs.

It is not a leap to go from the extant research on quality in traditional and distance education in Chapters Four and Five to the lists of best practices. And although the guidelines or best practices are based on some research, sometimes they are based on assumptions about quality that apply better to a more traditional education than to an on-line one. It is important to keep a critical eye on even the most well-worn truth or article of faith and continue to ask for the research specifically on on-line learning behind the recommendation.

Another valid criticism of the best practices approach to ensuring quality distance education is its trust that those who say they abide by the guidelines do so in every course and to good effect. If the best practices are actually being implemented, how would the prospective student or outsider know? What would be the evidence? And are there useful and viable exceptions to these guidelines? The danger may be that a set of guidelines is adopted too soon, codifying appropriate practice and thereby closing off continued improvements.

Unfortunately, no one set of guidelines (or even all taken together) may ensure quality. Evidence for quality may need to be developed case by case, be drawn from a variety of sources, and will—by its very nature—be messy and complicated and evolving.

Summary

This chapter reviewed the major sets of guidelines produced by WCET, CHEA, NEA, ITC, and CRAC, whose similarities and differences are appropriate to their clientele and primary interests. It also discussed some of the major faculty and student guides available, with a caveat on the dangers of relying too heavily on these guidelines.

Advice to the Confused

THIS CHAPTER DRAWS some words of advice for prospective students and parents—as well as faculty and institutions—on how to identify (and produce) a quality on-line course or program. It includes a discussion of new or revised measures of quality, two models for quality, the importance of certain attitudes and approaches to quality, ways to empower the consumer and use the guidelines in Chapter Six, and the persons with responsibility for quality. It closes with a final, hopeful note on what quality in on-line learning may become.

New Quality Measures

Obviously, accreditors, consumer protection agencies, and state regulators need new criteria for quality on-line learning. Institutions and faculty also need to know whether their efforts are resulting in a quality educational experience for students. Such criteria must focus first and foremost on student learning and be based on what is currently known from the research literature about contributors to success in on-line learning.

Some suggestions for criteria include such *input measures* as faculty qualifications (which may need to be broadened beyond content knowledge to include an understanding of instructional design), student learning styles, specific needs for on-line learning, and a grasp of what the Web can do (or what the Web-based courseware package can do). Faculty would also need an aptitude for, or experience with, teaching on-line, including a tolerance for failure and flexibility, willingness to learn and change, and an appreciation for their different role in learning (that is, moving from center stage to putting student learning at the center of the course). Institutions need to have extensive on-line resources to support student learning, including a library with an on-line catalogue, ability to send materials to distant students, and extensive on-line journals. A number of student services must be available via the Web to distant students: applications for admission and financial aid (that do not ask the student to print the form and mail it in); course and program information; course registration; advising of some nature; a way to view grades, order transcripts, and monitor progress toward graduation; a directory to services that goes beyond posting the phone numbers of offices open only from 8 A.M. to 5 P.M.; and the offer of special services on-line (e.g., veterans benefits, career advising, counseling). And as will become clear, faculty and institutions must have a real commitment to quality improvement and the assessment of student learning, including an emphasis on the evaluation of distance education programs and courses. Yet even with all these input measures in place, it should not be construed that quality exists or is assured, only that some preexisting conditions have been met.

Process measures include a description of processes for quality improvement for the individual class, the course, and the program. A variety of instructional models (and even a variety of instructional models within one course) or a matching of models to student learning styles and technology applications is necessary. Hallmarks of a quality Web-based course are ample opportunities for interaction between and among faculty and students and the course material. Each course should be designed to use the Web's ability to facilitate collaboration and community, to allow students to construct knowledge from experiences (whether real or simulated), and to help students apply knowledge, test it, and revise their understanding based on the application. The extent to which a course or program seriously attempts to develop higher intellectual functions rather than focusing on information transfer and to individualize learning experiences are two more measures of interest.

Thus, presumptions about some old process measures may be questioned. Faculty/student ratios may be less useful than before, as some open university courses enroll 10,000 students and produce undisputed student learning. Thinking about this ratio may be more useful if it is in terms of what is appropriate for the learning objectives of the course and the students' preparation or ability to undertake such learning. Faculty workload may need to be refined to recognize the additional time and effort required to develop new skills and courses (although as faculty gain experience and expertise, the workload may return to previous levels).

Outcome measures include measurable or qualitative student learning outcomes. Such outcomes would surely include content knowledge and relevant skills but might also include higher-level functions such as synthesis and analysis, creativity, and the development of new ideas or works. Given accreditors' interest in moving toward outcomes assessment in their review of institutions, each program and course should likely have designated outcomes and assessment techniques, including in-class tests, professional entry exams (if applicable), portfolios, and simulations. Most important to accreditors and faculty alike will be having a process for revising curricula based on the findings of the most recent assessments and a general attitude or willingness to ask tough questions of students and apply what is learned from the answers to teaching, courses, and the program as a whole.

To confirm the importance of defining and assessing outcomes, the Office of Postsecondary Education (U.S. Department of Education, 2000) stated that it would "encourage a strong focus on outcomes and competencies as measures of quality in distance education." This statement is mirrored by the results of a survey of campus stakeholders by Cleary (2001), who found that outcome indicators (e.g., pass rates on licensure exams, improvement of students' critical-thinking skills and writing skills) received the highest ranking for relevance. And despite the difficulty of defining and assessing student learning, higher education needs to "create a viable language and metric to demonstrate that learning has occurred" (Knight Higher Education Collaborative, 2000, p. 5).

Massy (2001, p. 50) has proposed seven core principles to make quality "work" (although they are not specifically about on-line learning):

1. Define quality in terms of outcomes.
2. Focus on the process of teaching and learning.
3. Strive for curricular coherence.

4. Work collaboratively to achieve mutual involvement and support.

5. Base decisions on facts, whenever possible.

6. Minimize controllable quality variations.

7. Make continuous quality improvement a top priority.

The continued chorus of interest in learning outcomes and continuous quality improvement is remarkable, and it sends a consistent message from a variety of constituencies to higher education institutions.

Although it may be obvious from this discussion, it is worth making explicit that no one measure—no one method—will be satisfactory for assessing quality. This point is made generally in the assessment literature, but it is made even more important when applied to the assessment of on-line learning (see Gunawardena, Lowe, and Carabajal, 2000).

Other Models of Quality

This section will review different models for Web-based learning that may provide some interesting and useful ways of defining a quality on-line course or program.

Holistic Model

Any conception of quality can and should recognize its holistic nature, where quality does not depend on a teaching tool, or a single learning style, or one activity. In this view, quality derives from many parts and evolves into something greater. Miller and Husmann (1996) have proposed a model of "program ecology" that is the multiplicative effect of course delivery, instructional quality, learner involvement, and course and program administration within the teaching and learning culture. This model is appealing, as it recognizes that quality is the result of many factors, which must be combined into a workable whole by students of on-line learning.

Fitness for Use

Another model for defining quality is based on "fitness for use," which can be defined from the point of view of the learner or other consumer (e.g., employer) as well as the faculty. Such a model would require a solid understanding of what "fitness for use" comprises in the life to be led by the student after graduation. It might include professional skills but also skills related to responsible citizenship and constructive interpersonal relationships. It sounds, on the face of it, like what colleges say they already do, but the perspectives of others are also important and must be sought. And it must be continually revised as conditions change and challenges evolve. This model would also require the development of quantitative and qualitative outcome measures and the assessment of learners at multiple points: before graduation and during the early career.

No question that this model is a difficult one to implement: it requires constant upgrading, continual evaluation of what is required to be "fit," new and possibly time-consuming assessments, and multiple applications of those assessments. It would be costly, at least at first. It would also be open to abuse: helping students prepare to fill narrow, employer-determined roles, roles that would be out-of-date in the four years it took students to complete their programs. This model also has a certain simplicity that is appealing, however, and it asks an important question that each institution should ask: How do students' experiences with on-line learning impact their lives?

No "One Size Fits All"

Some proponents of distance education have supported it as the alternative to a one-size-fits-all traditional education characterized by lectures and classes that require all students to meet in one place at one time and do one thing, largely in response to faculty directives. If the review of research tells us one thing, it is that far too many individual variables affect one's perception of quality (or experience of quality) for one single definition of quality. Calls for a definition of quality—as if one term or test or concept could do it—are misguided.

For example, Alley and Jansak (2001) found a lack of agreement among students, faculty, and administrators about what components were required for a good course. This lack of consensus may be the result of the range of individual factors that impact learning, different perceptions of what a good course is, and different experiences with a variety of learning approaches.

"I'll know a good course when I see it" may not be a satisfying definition of quality, but it may be closer to the truth of the situation.

Attitudes About Quality

In addition to understanding the implications of the various models for quality on-line learning, it is also important to realize the impact of various attitudes toward quality on the part of faculty and institutions.

Quality Improvement

Although assessment was mentioned earlier as part of the discussion on outcome measures, it is important to reassert its importance again as an approach and attitude toward quality. It is fundamental to the assessment movement that assessment be undertaken to help faculty and institutions improve the quality of student learning as they evaluate and modify curriculum, teaching strategies, materials, and assignments. Institutions with active, vibrant programs of assessment are more likely to have a positive attitude toward quality improvement.

The North Central Association Commission on Institutions of Higher Education began its Academic Quality Improvement Project (AQIP) (see http://www.aqip.org) in 2000 in an effort to design a "new approach to accreditation, based on quality improvement principles, values, and tools." The project will build a network of persons and institutions committed to quality improvement and developing a "quality culture" on individual campuses. AQIP focuses on a "web of common values—Focus, Involvement, Leadership, Learning, People, Collaboration, Agility, Foresight, Information, and Integrity" (Academic Quality Improvement Project, 2000, p. 3)—to build a systemic approach to continuous quality improvement. Involvement in this process is voluntary, and interested institutions must join the project and develop a contract between the institution and the North Central Association. Institutions may also exit from the AQIP and return to traditional accreditation processes. Major differences between the traditional and AQIP process of accreditation are that AQIP occurs on a three- to five-year cycle (compared with a ten-year cycle for traditional accreditation) and that AQIP requires a self-assessment and plan for improvement (compared with the self-study and formal accreditation visit of traditional processes). A think tank will test ways to drive quality improvement through higher education, and AQIP will provide such support services to institutions as colloquia on quality improvement involving other institutions in AQIP, recognition of outstanding practices, and consultant assistance for specific problems.

The AQIP quality criteria are largely systemic and focus on defining and evaluating processes that contribute to student learning. The process begins with "understanding students' and other stakeholders' needs." Five intermediating processes include "valuing people," "leading and communicating," "supporting institutional operations," "planning continuous improvement," and "building collaborative relationships." Two outcome areas include "helping students learn" and "accomplishing other distinctive objectives." Essential to the focus on student learning is the development of quantitative measures (against which to assess improvements in learning over time) that can be applied to both distance and traditional education, although other measures for important processes (e.g., teaching, research on learning, use of technology, responsive programs) are also included in the final assessment of how an institution is accomplishing its main objective.

Instructional Design

A quality on-line course benefits from a sharper understanding of the role of instructional design and its application to the students and material being taught. Students would benefit from investigating the attitude of faculty and the institution toward instruction and, particularly, whether they have a thorough understanding of instructional design and can choose among multiple pedagogical models.

Faculty need to eschew blaming the Web for failures if their choices on how to use it created a poor learning experience. Complaints about student isolation must force us to ask whether the faculty chose not to use the Web's capability to facilitate community and communication. If students are bored, have

Faculty need to eschew blaming the Web for failures if their choices on how to use it created a poor learning experience.

the faculty used the Web to post long pieces of text and ignored its ability to allow connections to visual or interactive material, let alone conversation areas to discuss the material with other students? If students drop out or become disengaged, is their disappearance a result of complicating events in their lives, poor learning, or the lack of communication with faculty and other students? We can no longer ignore the results shown in Reeves and Nass (1996), whose research implies that technologies such as the Web are useful to the extent faculty recognize the importance of good instruction and the psychological needs of the student interacting through the computer with course material and with other humans.

Research is needed, surely, and many areas for fruitful research are identified throughout this review of literature. But progress will be made once it is understood that quality may be determined by the instructional design of the course or program, not by the technologies used. Future research must distinguish between the instructional design and qualities of the Web.

Empowering the Consumer

As Twigg (2001b) pointed out, answering questions about quality requires one to ask from whose perspective we are considering quality (p. 1). If the perspective is that of a higher education institution, one might well respond with a list of measures not very different from those used in the past. If the perspective is that of consumers—with consumers defined as students, students' parents, or graduates' current or future employers—the answer might well be very different. For consumers, and those concerned for the safety and finances of consumers, the answer is information and, more specifically, comparative information.

In 1997–98, 54,470 distance learning courses were offered (National Center for Education Statistics, 1999b), which, given the rapid development of new courses, is likely a low number today. In one search alone, for a course in marketing, the results numbered 240 undergraduate courses, what Twigg (2001b) calls a "firehose of information." Despite this overwhelming amount of information, the student is left with many pertinent questions: What are the prerequisites for the course? What does it cover? Will face-to-face meetings be required?

The approach being proposed by Twigg (2001b) is to recognize that consumers may not need or want the best course, but the course that satisfies their most prevalent needs. This difference is an interesting departure from the higher education viewpoint, which emphasizes quality, when consumers are looking for a course that is good enough for their purposes or needs. But how do consumers find the information they need to make this decision?

If technology has caused this explosion of new courses, then it can "contribute to the solution" (Twigg, 2001b, p. 17). The proposal is to use Web-based tools (much like those used at www.amazon.com, www.ebay.com, or www.zagat.com) to allow consumers to search for courses based on individual preferences, to read an expert's point of view, and to provide advice to and receive information from other consumers. Given faculty reluctance to have student evaluations used in evaluations of their teaching, however, such a system might face opposition from faculty organizations.

On the face of it, this system could perpetuate misinformation or the sharing of bad advice. What is also needed is a concerted attempt to educate the consumer on what constitutes a quality education: a challenging curriculum, difficult questions to solve, the necessity to meet deadlines and high standards of performance, and skill in writing, thinking, and working with others. It will not, however, prevent students wanting an easy experience from seeking one out, and no amount of wishing it were otherwise will change that.

On the other hand, Twigg's approach (2001b) offers another view of quality that might be useful for institutions to consider: quality as defined by institutions is of less importance than a course that is good enough for students' needs. To some, that view sounds like a direct attack on the prerogatives and judgment of faculty, but to others, it is the sound of students voting with their feet. It is, at heart, a recognition that quality is in the eye of the beholder, and the most immediate beholder is the student. Whether civilization crumbles as a result of this change (as some might contend) or there is an evolving definition of quality, only time will tell.

Using the Guidelines

The formal adoption of one of the sets of guidelines (see Chapter Six) may not be sufficient for ensuring quality. Guidelines are especially useful if they are seen as a road map to unfamiliar territory; they help one navigate the road system, but having the map does not guarantee a timely arrival. And although the different sets of guidelines seem to be based on good sense and an understanding of current best practice, they are not always based on research that has investigated whether that understanding continues to apply to on-line courses. This is not intended to be a criticism of the guidelines, which are generally sound, but as a caution to accepting them without continued evaluation of each recommendation.

On the other hand, the guidelines may provide a necessary framework for reviewing each program's or institution's evidence to see whether, and to what extent, the guidelines have been taken seriously and implemented throughout the curriculum. It may be that an institution has adopted a set of guidelines but does not have the commitment to implement them or cannot implement them with current resources. Adoption, in this case, is no assurance of quality to the consumer but a well-meaning ruse. Evidence that the guidelines have been implemented would be a better guide for the student. In a joint document, the eight regional accrediting associations developed a draft statement and guidelines for distance-delivered programs. The document (www.wiche.edu/telecom/Guidelines.htm) details examples of types of evidence that may be pertinent, although additional types of evidence may be possible and should be sought.

It is extremely important that the guidelines (whichever set are adopted) do not devolve into a bible of inviolable rules. Given the evolution of the body of research on Web-based learning and the way our understanding changes, modifies earlier concepts, and leaps ahead into new areas, it would be a shame if these earlier attempts to set some ground rules were concretized and adopted as policy. There is nothing more difficult to change than outdated or counterproductive policies, especially if there are few new rules to replace the old policies. Leaving things open—encouraging experimentation and constant evaluation—may be better for supporting the evolution of quality on-line learning than a premature adoption of any one set of guidelines.

Responsibility for Quality

Massy (2001) recommends making quality the "work" of the faculty, yet is this not already the case? Twigg (1999) is mystified about the "obsessive concern about quality assurance in distance education." Even when a student is "eyeball-to-eyeball with us in a classroom," how do we know what they have learned? Twigg's point is that college faculty, who teach these on-line and distance education courses, are the "ones making judgments about whether or not students are learning." Indeed, put most simply, college-level learning is "what college faculty say it is," and it is the individual and unique responsibility of faculty to evaluate what and how well the student has learned.

What is reassuring from the case studies and individual personal reports is the number of faculty who begin skeptical of on-line learning but test it as part of a course or as a full-fledged distance education course. Most exit the experience having some or most of their fears allayed, and many are willing to repeat the experience, albeit with many ideas for improving the course next time around. It is the incremental improvements made by faculty based on evaluations of student learning that have the greatest potential for creating quality learning experiences for future on-line students. This approach emphasizes the importance of the "scholarship of teaching" proposed by Boyer (1990) and supported by Massy and Wilger (1996). Ultimately, it is the responsibility of faculty to define quality, ensure that students experience it, and hold themselves accountable for student learning, whether by on-line, Web-based experiences or in that elusive, "traditional" classroom.

Quality Education

Perhaps as the research continues to be compiled, it will be recognized that Web-based distance education can produce quality learning and that it can no longer be considered a separate entity, suspiciously different from its on-campus cousin but simply another form of, or venue for, education. Tait and Mills (1999) have documented the number and variety of ways distance and conventional education have "converged," not making the two the same but blurring the former distinctions between them. Perhaps in time on-line learning will have proved its worth and will have done so to the extent that its characteristics have been adopted into more traditional courses and environments.

As time passes, a variety of outcome measures will be evaluated, and it is likely that student achievement, test scores, or other performance measures will continue to be useful. On the other hand, more traditional markers for quality (e.g., contact hours, faculty/student ratio) will pass into disuse. The technology used (whether lecture on campus, Web-based, or some mixed model) will count less than whether a student can demonstrate the learning outcomes—the skills, knowledge, and competencies—set out for them by the program faculty.

And perhaps some day it will be generally agreed that it is not so much the technology that impacts student learning but the instructional design—the learning model—and the values implicit in the activities and content chosen by the faculty that determine whether the student learns or not. This conclusion is not novel, but perhaps it requires being said again, with feeling, that the Web is a tool—a very flexible tool—that is a means to an end. Whether the tool works well is the result of the user of the tool and his or her skill and assumptions. And even if, in time, we discover that the Web has certain clearly identifiable and distinct effects, we must wonder whether it will be as influential as the instructional model or other factors. In any case, it is the responsibility of faculty, and the institutions that enable their work, to learn how to use the Web well, to continue the work of understanding how students learn, and to discover how the Web can best be used to support that learning.

Conclusions

IT IS DIFFICULT TO JUSTIFY firm conclusions about many of the issues treated by the research studies reviewed in this report. Certain tentative conclusions can be made, however, based on what we know from the research so far.

First, there is no single, simple definition of quality (Chapter Three). Quality is a complex and difficult concept, one that depends on a range of factors arising from the student, the curriculum, the instructional design, technology used, faculty characteristics, and so on. Given the evidence on all the individual differences that affect student learning on-line, understanding and achieving quality on-line learning may be very complicated and may never yield one best way to ensure learning (Chapter Four). Quality probably results when there is an optimal match between learner and education, each bringing multiple aspects to the relationship that may encourage learning or make it more difficult to achieve. People do learn in all sorts of situations, however—sometimes in very poor environments—so it is important to realize that learning often occurs *despite* less than optimal conditions. In the final analysis, the conversation about quality and distance education would be more productive if it focused on uncovering ways to help students learn, irrespective of their location or whether technology is used.

Second, sound evidence exists that one of the more powerful contributors to student learning is multiple and various types of interaction: with the course material, with other students, and with faculty (Chapter Four). This evidence explains why uses of the Web that stress passive learning (such as reading large blocks of static material on-line) are less satisfactory. And although some proportion of students may prefer and do well with self-paced, solitary learning, the majority of students do better when they have ample opportunities to work with others. It may also explain the effectiveness of the various action-oriented educational approaches, including active learning, problem-based learning, and experiential learning, that derive from constructivist learning theory (Chapter Three). That means that courses offered on-line that do not allow ample opportunities to interact with other people (students, faculty, or experts) may be less effective for most students. Ultimately, the need for interaction with others may also justify retaining, and explain the continued popularity of, semester-based courses that continue to group students with faculty within a specific time frame.

Third, ample evidence exists that one of the most powerful and unintended consequences of the adoption of Web-based learning has been a resurgence of interest among faculty in learning theory, instructional design, and pedagogical techniques (Chapter Five). This outcome is most welcome, and it is one that may well spell the renewal of interest in Boyer's scholarship of teaching (1990) among college and university faculty and the improvement of instructional practice in both distance education and on-campus college-level classes.

Fourth, perhaps one of the most telling characteristics of a quality educational program may be an attitude—a value, belief, or goal—on the part of faculty and the institution for constant improvement and experimentation (Chapter Seven). In fact, using the Web requires a willingness to experiment and occasionally fail. An institution or faculty that is satisfied with current approaches may miss how students—and the skills they will need in the future—are changing. It seems that a lively, robust focus on student learning assessment encourages a positive attitude toward improvement by asking whether learning occurred and why. Further, it appears that only by focusing on assessment of student learning can we put to rest the doubts or worries about Web-based learning.

Fifth, perhaps it is important at this point to admit that there are probably institutions, faculty, and students who are not suited to on-line learning (Chapters Four and Five). There is no shame in this admission, nor is there any reason to belittle on-line learning if it does not suit every person or situation. In addition, it may someday be proved that on-line learning is more suited to some disciplines or learning objectives than others, although no evidence supports this speculation at this time. In fact, the imagination, creativity, and inventiveness of some on-line applications already developed tend to support the view that what some deemed impossible is only a year away from being solved. When in doubt, always bet on human resourcefulness.

Sixth, using a set of guidelines is certainly appropriate in the early stages of developing on-line learning experiences (Chapter Six). We must guard against seeing those guidelines become entrenched or writ in stone, however, slowing down further innovation and closing off the pursuit of further improvements and new understanding of what works best.

Seventh, we clearly need more research to answer some of our continuing questions about what works in on-line learning and why (Chapters Three, Four, and Five). Fortunately, faculty have adopted on-line learning in large numbers. And if the number of articles, conference presentations, and on-line discussions reviewed as part of this report is any indication, faculty have enormous interest in doing this research, engaging in hearty discussions, and thinking deeply and creatively about students' on-line learning. It would help, of course, if more resources were available to support the research that is so desperately needed, from federal sources or foundations. Monetary support is essential to make large-scale, complex research projects as well as longitudinal research a reality.

Eighth, perhaps after all the research is completed, it will be recognized that on-line learning is not so different after all. We may well conclude, as did G. Brown and Johnson-Shull (2000) that "good teaching is good teaching" and everything learned about good teaching, good instructional models, or being a good student is no different in the on-line setting (Chapter Seven). At this moment of realization, on-line learning and distance education may be just *education,* sharing the same qualities, theoretical constructs, and research base as its more traditional (although rapidly changing) campus-based twin. When it happens, there will be few questions about quality in distance education, only quality, however defined.

Last, the use of on-line learning—whether in distance education or on-campus courses—will likely continue to grow (Chapter One). Institutions may see it as a way to reach more students, faculty view it as a way to improve what they do, and students want it because it works for them. In any case, on-line learning is here to stay.

References

Abernathy, D. J. (1999). www.online.learning. *Training and Development, 52*(9), 36–41.

Academic Quality Improvement Project. (2000). NCA Academic Quality Improvement Project. [http://www.aqip.org/doc/AQIPbook.pdf]

Alley, L. R., and Jansak, K. E. (2001). Ten keys to quality assurance and assessment in online learning. [http://www.worldclassstrategies.com/papers/keys.htm]

Altany, A. (2000). The art of learning with technology: Spiritual, mystical and paradoxical memories of the future. [http://leahi.kcc.hawaii.edu/org/tcon2K/paper/paper_altanya.html]

American Association of University Professors. (2001a). Committee R on government relations report on distance learning. [http://www.aaup.org/statements/Redbook/DLREPORT.HTM]

American Association of University Professors. (2001b). Statement on distance learning. [http://www.aaup.org/Issues/DistanceEd/StDistEd.HTM]

American Center for the Study of Distance Education. (1999). Internet-based distance education bibliography. [http://www.ed.psu.edu/acsde/annbib/partb.asp]; [http://www.ed.psu.edu/acsde/annbib/partc.asp]

American Council on Education. (2001). Distributed education and its challenges: An overview. Washington, DC: American Council on Education.

American Federation of Teachers. (2000). Distance education: Guidelines for good practice. [http://www.aft.org/higher_ed/downloadable/distance.pdf]

American Federation of Teachers. (2001). Virtual revolution: Trends in the expansion of distance education. Washington, DC: American Federation of Teachers.

Anderson, T., Rourke, L., Garrison, D. R., and Archer, W. (2001). Assessing teaching presence in a computer conferencing context. *Journal of Asynchronous Learning Networks, 5*(2), 1–17.

Arbaugh, J. B. (2001). How instructor immediacy behaviors affect student satisfaction and learning in web-based courses. *Business Communication Quarterly, 64*(4), 42–54. [http://www.alnresearch.org/data_files/articles/full_text/arbaugh01.pdf]

Arvan, L., and Musumeci, D. (2000). Instructor attitudes within the SCALE efficiency projects. *Journal of Asynchronous Learning Networks, 4*(3). [http://www.aln.org/alnweb/journal/Vol4_issue3/fs/arvan/fs-arvan.htm]

Barker, K. (2001). Creating quality guidelines for on-line education and training. [http://www.futured.com]

Barone, C. A., and Hagner, P. R. (Eds.). (2001). *Technology-mediated teaching and learning.* San Francisco: Jossey-Bass.

Barr, R. B., and Tagg, J. (1995). From teaching to learning. *Change, 27*(6), 13–25.

Baxter, J. T., and Miller, M. T. (1998). Graduate education on the Internet: An issue of quality and accessibility. (ED 423 736)

Baylen, D. M., and Tyler, J. M. (1998). Making a beeline to becoming on-line: A case study. [http://leahi.kcc.hawaii.edu/org/tcon98/paper/baylen.html]

Becker, D., and Dwyer, M. (1998). The impact of student verbal/visual learning style preference on implementing groupware in the classroom. *Journal of Asynchronous Learning Networks, 2*(2). [http://www.aln.org/alnweb/journal/vol2_issue2/becker.htm]

Bellcourt, M. A. (1998). The humanity of technology. [http://leahi.kcc.hawaii.edu/org/tcon98/paper/bellcourt.html]

Benbunan-Fich, R., Hiltz, S. R., and Turoff, M. (2001). A comparative content analysis of face-to-face vs. ALN-mediated teamwork. [http://www.alnresearch.org/Data_Files/articles/abstract/abs_benbunan01.htm]

Berge, Z. L. (1997). Characteristics of online teaching in post-secondary, formal education. *Educational Technology, 37*(3), 35–47.

Berge, Z. L. (1998). Barriers to online teaching in post-secondary institutions: Can policy changes fix it? *Online Journal of Distance Learning Administration, 1*(2). [http://www.westga.edu/~distance/Berge12.html]

Berge, Z. L., and Mrozowski, S. (2001). Review of research in distance education, 1990–1999. *American Journal of Distance Education, 15*(3), 5–19.

Berns, R. G., and Erickson, P. M. (2001). Contextual teaching and learning: Preparing students for the new economy. [http://nccte.com/publications/infosynthesis/highlightzone/highlight05/highlight05-CTL.html]

Bernt, F. L., and Bugbee, A. C. (1993). Study of practices and attitudes related to academic success in a distance learning programme. *Distance Education, 14*(1), 97–112.

Betts, K. S. (1998). An institutional overview: Factors influencing faculty participation in distance education in postsecondary education in the United States: An institutional study. *Online Journal of Distance Learning Administration, 1*(3). [http://www.westga.edu/~distance/betts13.html]

Biner, P. M., Bink, M. L., Huffman, M. L., and Dean, R. S. (1995). Personality characteristics differentiating and predicting the achievement of televised-course students and traditional-course students. *American Journal of Distance Education, 9*(2), 46–60.

Bleck, B. (1999). Distance education with a heart: Getting to the MOO of the matter. [http://www.ccsn.nevada.edu/english/bleck/cw99paper.htm]

Bleck, B. (2000). John Dewey's "educative experience" and MOOs as learning environments. [http://leahi.kcc.hawaii.edu/org/tcon2k/paper/paper_bleckb.html]

Blum, K. D. (1999). Gender differences in asynchronous learning in higher education: Learning styles, participation barriers and communication patterns. *Journal of Asynchronous Learning Networks, 3*(1). [http://www.aln.org/alnweb/journal/jaln_vol3issue1.html]

Boaz, M., and others. (1999). Teaching at a distance: A handbook for instructors. Mission Viejo, CA: League for Innovation in the Community College.

Boettcher, J. V., and Conrad, R. (1999). Faculty guide for moving teaching and learning to the web. Mission Viejo, CA: League for Innovation in the Community College.

Bothun, G. D. (1998). Distance education: Effective learning or content-free credits? *Cause/Effect, 21*(2), 28–36.

Bourne, J. R., McMaster, E., Rieger, J., and Campbell, J. O. (1997). Paradigms for on-line learning. *Journal of Asynchronous Learning Networks, 1*(2). [http://www.aln.org/alnweb/journal/issue2/assee.htm]

Boyer, E. L. (1990). *Scholarship reconsidered: Priorities of the professoriate.* San Francisco: Jossey-Bass.

Brooks, D. (1997). Web-teaching: *A guide to interactive teaching for the World Wide Web.* New York: Plenum Press.

Brown, B. L. (1997). New learning strategies for Generation X. ERIC Clearinghouse on Adult, Career, and Vocational Education. [http://www.ericacve.org/docgen.asp?tbl= digests&ID=37]

Brown, B. L. (1998). Applying constructivism in vocational and career education. ERIC Clearinghouse on Adult, Career, and Vocational Education. [http://www.ericacve.org/ mp_brown_01.asp]

Brown, B. L. (2000). Web-based training. ERIC Clearinghouse on Adult, Career, and Vocational Education. [http://www.ericacve.org/docgen.asp?tbl=digests&ID=103]

Brown, G. (2000, January/February). Where do we go from here? *Technology Source.* [http://horizon.unc.edu/TS/default.asp?show=article&id=667]

Brown, G., and Johnson-Shull, L. (2000, May/June). Teaching online: Now we're talking. *Technology Source.* [http://horizon.unc.edu/TS/default.asp?show=article&id=676]

Brown, G., and Wack, M. (1999a, May/June). The difference frenzy and matching buckshot with buckshot. *Technology Source.* [http://horizon.unc.edu/TS/default.asp?show=article&id=667]

Brown, G., and Wack, M. (1999b, April). Online collaboration and implications for learning and society. *Technology Source.* [http://horizon.unc.edu/TS/reading/1999-04.asp]

Brown, J. S. (2000). Growing up digital. *Change, 32*(2), 11–20.

Brown, J. S., and Duguid, P. (2000). *The social life of information.* Cambridge, MA: Harvard Business School Press.

Brown, R. E. (2001). The process of community-building in distance learning classes. *Journal of Asynchronous Learning Networks, 5*(2), 18–35.

Buchanan, E. A. (1999). Assessment measures: Pre-tests for successful distance teaching and learning? *Online Journal of Distance Learning Administration, 2*(4). [http://www.westga.edu/~distance/buchanan24.html]

Burbules, N. C., and Callister, T. A. (2000). Universities in transition: The promise and the challenge of new technologies. *Teachers College Record, 102*(2), 271–293. [http://www.tcrecord.org/Content.asp?ContentID=10362]

Bures, E. M., Abrami, P. C., and Amundsen, C. (2000). Student motivation to learn via computer conferencing. *Research in Higher Education, 41*(5), 593–621.

Campos, M., and Harasim, L. M. (1999, July/August). Virtual-U: Results and challenges of unique field trials. *Technology Source.* [http://horizon.unc.edu/TS/default.asp?show=article&id=562]

Campos, M., Laferrière, T., and Harasim, L. (2001). The post-secondary networked classroom: Renewal of teaching practices and social interaction. *Journal of Asynchronous Learning Networks, 5*(2), 36–52.

Cárdenas, K. (1998). Technology in today's classroom: It slices and it dices, but does it serve us well? *Academe, 84*(3), 27–29.

Carr, S. (2000, June 23). Publishers rush to offer distance-education information in print. *Chronicle of Higher Education.* [http://www.chronicle.com/free/2000/06/2000062301u.htm]

Cennamo, K. S., Ross, J. D., and Rogers, C. S. (2002). Evolution of a web-enhanced course. *Educause Quarterly, 25*(1), 28–33.

Center for Occupational Research and Development. (2001). What is contextual learning? [http://www.cord.org/Lev2.cfm/56]

Cerny, M. G., and Heines, J. M. (2001). Evaluating distance education across twelve time zones. *T.H.E. Journal, 28*(7). [http://www.thejournal.com/magazine/vault/A3296.cfm]

Chickering, A. W., and Ehrmann, S. C. (1996). Implementing the seven principles: Technology as lever. [http://www.aahe.org/technology/ehrmann.htm]

Chickering, A. W., and Gamson, Z. (1987, May). Seven principles of good practice in undergraduate education. *AAHE Bulletin,* 3–7. (ED 282 491)

Clark, R. E. (1994). Media will never influence learning. *Educational Technology Research and Development, 42*(2), 21–29.

Cleary, T. S. (2001). Indicators of quality. *Planning for Higher Education, 29*(3), 19–28.

Coppola, N. W., Hiltz, S. R., and Rotter, N. (2001). Becoming a virtual professor. [http://www.alnresearch.org/Data_Files/articles/abstract/abs_coppola01.html]

Council for Higher Education Accreditation. (1998). Assuring quality in distance learning. Washington, DC: Council for Higher Education Accreditation.

Council for Higher Education Accreditation. (2000). The competency standards project: Another approach to accreditation review. Occasional paper. Washington, DC: Council for Higher Education Accreditation.

Council of Regional Accrediting Commissions. (2000). Statement of the regional accrediting commissions on the evaluation of electronically offered degree and certificate programs and guidelines for the evaluation of electronically offered degree and certificate programs. [http://www.wiche.edu/wcet/resources/publications/guidelines.pdf]

Dataquest, Inc. (1999). Half of households have PC. [http://www.gartner.com]

Davies, R. S., and Mendenhall, R. (1998). Evaluation comparison of online and classroom instruction for HEPE 129-Fitness and Lifestyle Management course. (ED 427 752)

Dede, C. (1996). Emerging technologies and distributed learning. *American Journal of Distance Education, 10*(2), 4–36.

Dereshiwsky, M. I. (2000). The Ten Commandments of success in cyberinstruction. [http://leahi.kcc.hawaii.edu/org/tcon2k/paper/paper_dereshiwskym.html]

Diaz, D. P. (2000, March/April). Carving a new path for distance education research. *Technology Source.* [http://horizon.unc.edu/TS/default.asp?show=article&id=648]

Diaz, D. P. (2001, November/December). Taking technology to the classroom: Pedagogy-based training for educators. *Technology Source.* [http://ts.mivu.org/default.asp?show=article&id=924]

Diaz, D. P., and Bontenbal, K. F. (2001). Learner preferences: Developing a learner-centered environment in the online mediated classroom. *ED at a Distance, 15*(8). [http://www.usdla.org/html/journal/AUG01_Issue/article03.html]

DiBiase, D. (2000). Is distance teaching more work or less work? *American Journal of Distance Education, 14*(3), 6–20.

Dille, B., and Mezack, M. (1991). Identifying predictors of high risk among community college telecourse students. *American Journal of Distance Education, 5*(1), 24–35.

Dillon, A., and Gabbard, R. (1998). Hypermedia as an educational technology: A review of the quantitative research literature on learner comprehension, control, and style. *Review of Educational Research, 68*(3), 322–349.

Dominguez, P. S., and Ridley, D. (1999). Reassessing the assessment of distance education courses. *T.H.E. Journal, 27*(2). [http://www.thejournal.com/magazine/vault/A2223.cfm]

Dziuban, C., and Moskal, P. (2001). Evaluating distributed learning at metropolitan universities. *Educause Quarterly, 24*(4), 60–61.

Dziuban, C. D., Moskal, P. D., and Dziuban, E. K. (2000). Reactive behavior patterns go online. *Journal of Staff, Program, and Organizational Development, 17*(3), 171–182.

Eaton, J. S. (2001). Distance learning: Academic and political challenges for higher education accreditation. Washington, DC: Council for Higher Education Accreditation.

Edelson, P. J. (2000). Virtual and face-to-face learning: Meeting points. (ED 442 934)

Edmonds, G. S. (1999, March). Making change happen: Planning for success. *Technology Source.* [http://horizon.unc.edu/TS/default.asp?show=article&id=40]

Educational Resources Information Center. (2001). Assessing learning online. [http://www.ericacve.org/docs/pfile03.htm]

Educause. (2001). Institutional readiness. [http://www.educause.edu/ready]

Ehrmann, S. C. (1997). Asking the right question: What does research tell us about technology and higher learning? [http://www.learner.org/edtech/rscheval/rightquestion.html]

Eklund, J., and Eklund, P. (1996). Integrating the web and the teaching of technology: Cases across two universities. [http://ausweb.scu.edu.au/aw96/educn/eklund2/paper.html]

Enomoto, E., and Tabata, L. (2000). Creating virtual learning communities through distance learning technologies: A course examined. [http://leahi.kcc.hawaii.edu/org/tcon2k/paper/paper_enomotoe.html]

Fahy, P. J. (2000). Achieving quality with online teaching technologies. (ED 439 234)

Farber, J. (1998). The third circle: On education and distance learning. *Sociological Perspectives, 41*(4), 797–814.

Fitzsimmons, J., and O'Brien, W. (2000). Online resistance: Learning learning modalities while studying the short story. [http://leahi.kcc.hawaii.edu/org/tcon2k/paper/paper_fitzsimmonsj.html]

Fjortoff, N. F. (1995). Predicting persistence in distance learning programs. (ED 387 620)

Flowers, L., Pascarella, E. T., and Pierson, C. T. (2000). Information technology use and cognitive outcomes in the first year of college. *Journal of Higher Education, 71*(6), 637–667.

Fredericksen, E., and others. (2000a). Factors influencing faculty satisfaction with asynchronous teaching and learning in the SUNY learning network. *Journal of Asynchronous Learning Networks, 4*(3). [http://www.aln.org/alnweb/journal/Vol4_issue3/fs/Fredericksen/fs-fredericksen.htm]

Fredericksen, E., and others. (2000b). Student satisfaction and perceived learning with on-line courses: Principles and examples from the SUNY learning network. *Journal of Asynchronous Learning Networks, 4*(2). [http://www.aln.org/alnweb/journal/Vol4_issue2/le/Fredericksen/LE-fredericksen.htm]

Gagne, M., and Shepherd, M. (2001). A comparison between a distance and a traditional graduate accounting class. *T.H.E. Journal, 28*(9). [http://www.thejournal.com/magazine/vault/A3433.cfm]

Gardner, H. (1983). *Frames of mind.* New York: Basic Books.

Gardner, H. (2000). *The disciplined mind.* New York: Penguin Books.

Garland, M. R. (1993). Student perceptions of the situational, institutional, dispositional, and epistemological barriers to persistence. *Distance Education, 14*(2), 181–198.

Garrison, D. R., Anderson, T., and Archer, W. (2001). Critical thinking, cognitive presence, and computer conferencing in distance education. *American Journal of Distance Education, 15*(1), 7–23.

Garrison, S. (1999). Dual perspectives on the effectiveness of project-based learning in an online environment. [http://leahi.kcc.hawaii.edu/org/tcon99/papers/garrison1.html]

Garrison, S., and Onken, M. H. (1998). Practical lessons on delivery of distance learning: Do's and don'ts. [http://leahi.kcc.hawaii.edu/org/tcon98/paper/onken.html]

Gen, R. (2000). Technology and multiple intelligences. *ED at a Distance, 15*(5). [http://www.usdla.org/html/journal/MAY00_Issue/index.htm]

Geoghegan, W. H. (1994). Whatever happened to instructional technology? Paper presented at the 22nd Annual Conference of the International Business Schools Computing Association, Baltimore, Maryland.

Gibson, C. C. (Ed.). (1997). *Distance learners in higher education: Institutional responses for quality outcomes.* Madison, WI: Atwood.

Gibson, C. G. (1990). Learners and learning: A discussion of selected research. In M. G. Moore (Ed.), *Contemporary Issues in American Distance Education* (pp. 121–135). New York: Pergamon Press.

Gibson, J., and Rutherford, P. (2000). Growing a natural classroom dynamic on the web. [http://leahi.kcc.hawaii.edu/org/tcon2k/paper/paper_gibsonj.html]

Gilbert, S. W., and Green, K. C. (1995). Information technology: A road to the future? (ED 404 924)

Gillespie, K. H. (Ed.). (1998). *The impact of technology on faculty development, life, and work.* New Directions for Teaching and Learning, no. 76. San Francisco: Jossey-Bass.

Girod, M., and Cavanaugh, S. (2001). Technology as an agent of change in teacher practice. *T.H.E. Journal, 28*(9). [http://www.thejournal.com/magazine/vault/A3429.cfm]

Gose, B. (1999, February 19). Surge in continuing education brings profits for universities. *Chronicle of Higher Education, 45*(24), A24. [http://www.chronicle.com/weekly/v45/i24/24a05101.htm (subscription required)]

Gould, S. J. (1981). *The mismeasure of man.* New York: Norton.

Graham, C., and others. (2001, March/April). Seven principles of effective teaching: A practical lens for evaluating online courses. *Technology Source.* [http://horizon.unc.edu/TS/default.asp?show=article&id=839]

Grasha, A. F. (1996). *Teaching with style.* Pittsburgh: Alliance.

Green, K. C. (2001). The Campus Computing Project: 2001 results. Claremont, CA: Claremont Graduate University. [http://www.campuscomputing.net]

Gross, R., Gross, D., and Pirkl, R. (1998). New connections: A guide to distance education. Washington, DC: Instructional Telecommunications Council.

Gunawardena, C. N., Lowe, C., and Carabajal, K. (2000). Evaluating online learning: Models and methods. (ED 444 552)

Gunawardena, C. N., and Zittle, F. J. (1997). Social presence as a predictor of satisfaction within a computer-mediated conferencing environment. *American Journal of Distance Education, 11*(3), 6–26.

Hagner, P. R., and Schneebeck, C. A. (2001). Engaging the faculty. In C. A. Barone and P. R. Hagner (Eds.), *Technology-mediated teaching and learning* (pp. 1–12). San Francisco: Jossey-Bass.

Hahn, H. A., and others. (1990). Distributed training for the reserve component: Remote delivery using asynchronous computer conferencing. (ED 359 918)

Hanna, D. E. (1998). Higher education in an era of digital competition: Emerging organizational models. *Journal of Asynchronous Learning Networks, 2*(1). [http://www.aln.org/alnweb/journal/Vol2_issue1/hanna.htm]

Hanson, R. E., and Jubeck, T. (1999). Assessing the effectiveness of web page support in a large lecture course. *DEOS News, 9*(9).

Harasim, L. (1987). Teaching and learning on-line: Issues in computer-mediated graduate courses. *Canadian Journal of Educational Communication, 16*(2), 117–135.

Harasim, L. (1989). On-line education: A new domain. In R. Mason and A. Kaye (Eds.) *Mindweave: Communication, computers, and distance education.* Oxford: Pergamon Press.

Harasim, L. (1995). Shaping cyberspace into human space. *CSS Update, 6*(3). [http://fas.sfu.ca/css/update/vol6/6.3-harasim.main.html]

Harasim, L., and others. (1996). *Learning networks.* Cambridge, MA: MIT Press.

Hartley, K., and Bendixen, L. D. (2001). Educational research in the Internet age: Examining the role of individual characteristics. *Educational Researcher, 30*(9), 22–26.

Hartman, J., Dziuban, C., and Moskal, P. (2000). Faculty satisfaction in ALNs: A dependent or independent variable? *Journal of Asynchronous Learning Networks, 4*(3). [http://www.aln.org/alnweb/journal/Vol4_issue3/fs/hartman/fs-hartman.htm]

Hartman, J., and Truman-Davis, B. (2001). Faculty satisfaction: An overview. *Online Education, 2,* 109–128.

Healy, J. M. (1999). *Failure to connect.* New York: Simon & Schuster.

Helgeson, S. L. (1988). Microcomputers in the science classroom. ERIC/SMEAC Science Education Digest, no. 3. (ED 309 050)

Henderikx, P. (1992). Management and promotion of quality in distance education. *Open Learning, 7*(3), 34–41.

Higher Education Research Institute. (1998). The American college teacher: 1998–99. [http://www.gseis.ucla.edu/heri/press_faculty.htm]

Hillman, D.C.A. (1999). A new method for analyzing patterns of interaction. *American Journal of Distance Education, 13*(2), 37–47.

Hiltz, S. R. (1997). Impacts of college-level courses via asynchronous learning networks: Some preliminary results. *Journal of Asynchronous Learning Networks, 1*(2). [http://www.aln.org/alnweb/journal/issue2/hiltz.htm]

Hiltz, S. R., Coppola, N., Trotter, N., and Turoff, M. (2000). Measuring the importance of collaborative learning for the effectiveness of ALN: A multi-measure, multi-method approach. *Journal of Asynchronous Learning Networks, 4*(2). [http://www.aln.org/alnweb/journal/Vol4_issue2/le/hiltz/le-hiltz.htm]

Hoffman, R. (2001, May). Technology's impact on the faculty: A perspective. Technology Source. [http://horizon.unc.edu/TS/default.asp?show=article&id=853]

Hohn, M. D. (1998). Why is change so hard? [http://gseweb.harvard.edu/~ncsall/fob/1998/hohn.htm]

Imel, S. (1999). Using technologies effectively in adult and vocational education. ERIC Clearinghouse on Adult, Career and Vocational Education. [http://www.ericacve.org/docgen.asp?tbl=pab&ID=92]

Imel, S. (2000). Contextual learning in adult education. ERIC Clearinghouse on Adult, Career and Vocational Education. [http://www.ericacve.org/docgen.asp?tbl=pab&ID=102]

Institute for Higher Education Policy. (2000). Quality on the line. Washington, DC: National Education Association.

Iowa Association of Independent Colleges and Universities. (1997). Consumer's guide to choosing college courses on the Internet. [http://www.drake.edu/iaicu/consumer_guide.html]

Jacobson, M. J., and Spiro, R. J. (1995). Hypertext learning environments, cognitive flexibility, and the transfer of complex knowledge: An empirical investigation. *Journal of Educational Computing Research, 12*(4), 301–303.

Jaffee, D. (1998). Institutionalized resistance to asynchronous learning networks. *Journal of Asynchronous Learning Networks, 2*(2). [www.aln.org/alnweb/journal/Vol2_issue2/jaffee.htm]

Johnson, S. M. (2001). Teaching introductory international relations in an entirely web-based environment: Comparing student performance across and within groups. *ED at a Distance, 15*(10). [http://www.usdla.org/html/journal/JAN01_Issue/index.html]

Jones, D. (1996). Solving some problems of university education: A case study. [http://ausweb.scu.edu.au/aw96/educn/jones/index.html]

Jones, D., Lindner, J. R., Murphy, T. H., and Dooley, K. E. (2002). Faculty philosophical position towards distance education: Competency, value, and educational technology support. *Online Journal of Distance Learning Administration, 5*(1). [http://www.westga.edu/~distance/ojdla/spring51/jones51.html]

Joy, E. H., and Garcia, F. E. (2000). Measuring learning effectiveness: A new look at no significant findings. *Journal of Asynchronous Learning Networks, 4*(1). [http://www.aln.org/alnweb/journal/jaln_vol4issue1/joygarcia.htm]

Kapinus, C. (2001, May/June). Combining technology and group learning. *Technology Source.* [http://horizon.unc.edu/TS/default.asp?show=article&id=851]

Katz, R. N. (1997). Higher education and the forces of self-organization: An interview with Margaret Wheatley. *Cause/Effect, 29*(1), 18–21.

Katz, R. N., and Associates. (1999). *Dancing with the devil.* San Francisco: Jossey-Bass.

Knight Higher Education Collaborative. (2000). The mission and the medium. *Policy Perspectives, 9*(3), 1–9.

Knowles, M. (1978). *The adult learner: A neglected species.* Houston: Gulf Publishing Company.

Kotter, J. P. (1996). *Leading change.* Boston: Harvard Business School Press.

Kovel-Jarboe, P. (1997). From the margin to the mainstream: State-level policy and planning for distance education. In C. L. Dillon and R. Cintrón (Eds.), *Building a working policy for distance education* (pp. 23–32). New Directions for Community Colleges, no. 99. San Francisco: Jossey-Bass.

Kozma, R. (1994a). A reply: Media and methods. *Educational Technology Research and Development, 42*(3), 11–14.

Kozma, R. (1994b). Will media influence learning? Reframing the debate. *Educational Technology Research and Development, 42*(2), 7–19.

Kuh, G., and Vesper, N. (1999). Do computers enhance or detract from student learning? Paper presented at the annual meeting of the American Educational Research Association, Montreal, Quebec.

Lefoe, G., and Corderoy, R. M. (1998). Tips for effective online teaching and learning. [http://leahi.kcc.hawaii.edu/org/tcon98/paper/lefoe.html]

Lenhart, A. (2000). Who's not online. Washington, DC: Pew Internet and American Life Project.

Levinson, P. (2001). *Digital McLuhan.* London: Routledge.

Lim, C. K. (2001). Computer self-efficacy, academic self-concept, and other predictors of satisfaction and future participation of adult distance learners. *American Journal of Distance Education, 15*(2), 41–51.

Liu, Y., and Ginther, D. (1999). Cognitive styles and distance education. *Online Journal of Distance Learning Administration, 2*(3). [http://www.westga.edu/~distance/liu23.html]

Lockee, B. B., Burton, J. K., and Cross, L. H. (1999). New use for "no significant difference." *Educational Technology Research and Development, 7*(3), 33–42.

Loomis, K. D. (2000). Learning styles and asynchronous learning: Comparing the LASSI model to class performance. *Journal of Asynchronous Learning Networks, 4*(1). [http://www.aln.org/alnweb/journal/Vol4_issue1/loomis.htm]

Lynch, M. M. (2001, November/December). Effective student preparation for online learning. *Technology Source.* [http://ts.mivu.org/default.asp?show=article&id=901]

Mabrito, M. (1998). Local versus global computer conferences: Case studies of apprehensive writers. [http://leahi.kcc.hawaii.edu/org/tcon98/paper/mabrito.html]

Marchese, T. J. (2000). The new conversations about learning. [http://www.aahe.org/pubs/TM-essay.htm]

Mason, R., and Weller, M. (2001). Factors affecting students' satisfaction on a web course. *ED at a Distance, 15*(80). [http://www.usdla.org/html/journal/AUG01_Issue/article02.html]

Massy, W. (2001). Making quality work. *University Business 4*(6), 44–48.

Massy, W. F., and Wilger, A. K. (1996). It's time to redefine quality. Palo Alto, CA: Stanford Institute for Higher Education Research, Stanford University.

Massy, W. F., and Zemsky, R. (1995). Using information technology to enhance academic productivity. Washington, DC: Educom.

Mayer, R. E. (2001). *Multi-media learning.* Cambridge, UK: Cambridge University Press.

McLuhan, M. (1964). *Understanding media.* New York: McGraw-Hill.

McNeil, D. R., and others. (1991). Computer conferencing project. Final report. (ED 365 307)

Mellow, G. O., Sokenu, J., and Lynch-Donohue, B. (1998). Integrating technology into the classroom: Exploring what it means for faculty and students. *Community College Journal, 68*(7), 24–30.

Mezirow, J. (1991). *Transformative dimensions of adult learning.* San Francisco: Jossey-Bass.

Miller, B. (2000). Comparison of large-class instruction versus online instruction: Age does make a difference. [http://leahi.kcc.hawaii.edu/org/tcon2k/paper/paper_millerb.html]

Miller, M. D., and Corley, K. (2001). The effect of e-mail messages on student participation in the asynchronous on-line course: A research note. *Online Journal of Distance Learning Administration, 4*(3). [http://www.westga.edu/~distance/ojdla/fall43/miller43.html]

Miller, M. T., and Husmann, D. E. (1996). A holistic model for primary factors in the ecology of distance education course offerings. *Journal of Distance Education, 11*(1), 101–110.

Milliron, M. D., and Miles, C. L. (1998). Technology, learning, and community (TLC). Mission Viejo, CA: League for Innovation in the Community College.

Mingle, J. R. (1998). New technology funds: Problem or solution? STATE Lines. [http://sheeo.org/SHEEO/pubs-agb-tech.html]

Moore, M. G. (1990). Background and overview of contemporary American distance education. In M. G. Moore (Ed.), *Contemporary issues in American distance education* (pp. 1–25). New York: Pergamon Press.

Moore, M. G. (1997). Lessons from history. *American Journal of Distance Education, 11*(1), 1–5.

Moore, M. G. (1998). Quality in distance education: Four cases. *American Journal of Distance Education, 11*(3), 1–7.

Moore, M. G., and Cozine, G. T. (2000). Web-based communications, the Internet, and distance education. University Park: American Center for the Study of Distance Education, Pennsylvania State University.

Moore, M. G., and Kearsley, G. (1996). *Distance education: A systems view.* Belmont, CA: Wadsworth.

Moore, M. G., and Thompson, M. M. (1997). The effects of distance learning. ACSDE Research Monograph, no. 15. University Park: American Center for the Study of Distance Education, Pennsylvania State University.

Morgan, C., and O'Reilly, M. (1999). *Assessing open and distance learners.* London: Kogan Page.

Morley, J. (2000). Methods of assessing learning in distance education courses. *ED at a Distance, 13*(1). [http://www.usdla.org/html/journal/JAN00_Issue/Methods.htm]

Morrison, G. R. (2001). Theory, research and practice. *ED at a Distance, 15*(40). [http://www.usdla.org/html/journal/APR01_Issue/article06.html]

Morrison, J. L. (1999). The role of technology in education today and tomorrow: An interview with Kenneth Green, part 2. *On The Horizon, 7*(1). [http://horizon.unc.edu/horizon/online/html/7/1/editor.asp]

Morrison, J. L. (2000, May/June). E-learning and educational transformation: An interview with Greg Priest. *Technology Source.* [http://horizon.unc.edu/TS/vision/2000-05.asp]

Muilenburg, L., and Berge, Z. L. (2001). Barriers to distance education: A factor-analytic study. *American Journal of Distance Education, 15*(2), 7–22.

Muirhead, B. (2001). Enhancing social interaction in computer-mediated distance education. *ED at a Distance, 15*(40). [http://www.usdla.org/html/journal/APR01_Issue/article02.html]

Mulligan, R., and Geary, S. (1999). Requiring writing, ensuring distance-learning outcomes. *International Journal of Instructional Media, 26*(4), 387–395.

Murphy, E. (1997). Constructivism: From philosophy to practice. [http://www. stemnet.nf.ca/~elmurphy/emurphy/cle.html]

National Center for Education Statistics. (1999a). Digest of educational statistics. [http://nces.ed.gov/pubs2001/digest/dt418.html]

National Center for Education Statistics. (1999b). Distance education at postsecondary education institutions: 1997–98. [http://nces.ed.gov/pubsearch/pubsinfo.asp?pubid_00013]

National Center for Education Statistics. (2002). Distance education instruction by postsecondary faculty and staff: Fall 1998. [http://nces.ed.gov/pubs2002/2002155.pdf]

National Education Association. (1997). Going the distance: State legislative leaders talk about higher education and technology. Washington, DC: National Education Association.

National Governors Association. (1999). Transforming learning through technology. Santa Monica, CA: Milken Exchange.

National Governors Association. (2001a). The state of e-learning in the states. [http://www.nga.org/cda/files/060601elearning.pdf]

National Governors Association. (2001b). A vision of e-learning for America's workforce. [http://www.nga.org/cda/files/elearningreport.pdf]

National Telecommunications Information Agency. (1999). Falling through the net. [http://www.ntia.doc.gov/ntiahome/fttn99/execsummary.html]

Navarro, P., and Shoemaker, J. (2000). Performance and perceptions of distance learners in cyberspace. *American Journal of Distance Education, 14*(2), 15–35.

Neal, J. E. (1998). Quality assurance in the entrepreneurial university. In G. H. Gaither (Ed.), *Quality assurance in higher education: an international perspective* (pp. 69–85). New Directions for Institutional Research, no. 99. San Francisco: Jossey-Bass.

Nelson, G. (1998). Internet/web-based instruction and multiple intelligences. *Educational Media International, 35*(2), 90–94.

Newman, D. R., Webb, B., and Cochrane, C. (1999). A content analysis method to measure critical thinking in face-to-face and computer supported group learning. [http://www.qub.ac.uk/mgt/papers/methods/contpap.html]

Noakes, N. (1999). Collaboration and community constituents: An investigation into the key elements that build, nurture and sustain a collaborative learning community in networked spaces. [http://leahi.kcc.hawaii.edu/org/tcon99/papers/noakes.html]

Oblinger, D. G. (1998). Technology and change: Impossible to resist. *NCA Quarterly, 72*(4), 417–431.

Ory, J. C., Bullock, C., and Burnaska, K. (1997). Gender similarity in the use of and attitudes about ALN in a university setting. *Journal of Asynchronous Learning Networks, 1*(1).

Osborne, V. (2001). Identifying at-risk students in videoconferencing and web-based distance education. *American Journal of Distance Education, 15*(1), 41–54.

Palattella, J. (1998). The British are coming, the British are coming. *University Business, 1*(3), 125–130.

Palloff, R. M., and Pratt, K. (1999). *Building learning communities in cyberspace.* San Francisco: Jossey-Bass.

Parker, D., and Gemino, A. (2001). Inside online learning: Comparing conceptual and technique learning performance in place-based and ALN formats. *Journal of Asynchronous Learning Networks, 5*(2), 64–74.

Paskey, J. (2001, April 26). A survey compares two Canadian MBA programs, one online and one traditional. *Chronicle of Higher Education.* [http://chronicle.com/free/2001/04/2001042601u.htm]

Peha, J. M. (1997). Debates via computer networks: Improving writing and bridging classrooms. *T.H.E. Journal, 24*(9), 65–69. [http://www.thejournal.com/magazine/vault/A1366D.cfm]

Perrin, D. G. (2000). Supply chain management: Options for learning technologies. *ED at a Distance, 14*(4). [http://www.usdla.org/html/journal/APR00_Issue/supply%20chain.htm]

Phipps, R., and Merisotis, J. (1999). What's the difference? Washington, DC: Institute for Higher Education.

Phipps, R. A., Wellman, J. V., and Merisotis, J. P. (1998). Assuring quality in distance learning. Washington, DC: Council for Higher Education Accreditation.

Pimentel, J. R. (1999). Design of net.learning system based on experiential learning. *Journal of Asynchronous Learning Networks, 3*(2).

Presby, L. (2001). Increasing productivity in course delivery. *T.H.E. Journal, 28*(7). [http://www.thejournal.com/magazine/vault/A3298.cfm]

Primary Research Group. (1999). The survey of distance learning programs in higher education. New York: Primary Research Group.

Privateer, P. M. (1999). Academic technology and the future of higher education. *Journal of Higher Education, 70*(1), 60–79.

Quality Assurance Agency for Higher Education. (2000). Guidelines on the quality assurance of distance learning. [http://www.qaa.ac.uk/public/dlg/contents.htm]

Ragan, L. C. (1999). Good teaching is good teaching: An emerging set of guiding principles and practices for the design and development of distance education. *Cause/Effect, 22*(1). [http://www.educase.edu/ir/library/html/cem9915.html]

Reeves, B., and Nass, C. (1996). *The media equation.* Cambridge, UK: Cambridge University Press.

Roblyer, M. D., and Ekhaml, L. (2000). How interactive are YOUR distance courses? A rubric for assessing interaction in distance learning. *Online Journal of Distance Learning Administration, 3*(2). [http://www.westga.edu/~distance/roblyer32.html]

Rockwell, S. K., Schauer, J., Fritz, S. M., and Marx, D. B. (1999). Incentives and obstacles influencing higher education faculty and administrators to teach via distance. *Online Journal of Distance Learning Administration, 2*(4). [http://www.westga.edu/~distance/rockwell24.html]

Rogers, E. M. (1995). *Diffusion of innovations.* New York: Free Press.

Ruppert, S. S. (2000). A survey of traditional and distance learning higher education members. Washington, DC: Abacus Associates.

Russell, T. L. (1999). *The no significant difference phenomenon.* Raleigh: North Carolina State University.

Ryan, R. C. (2000). Student assessment comparison of lecture and online construction equipment and methods classes. *T.H.E. Journal, 27*(6). [http://www.thejournal.com/magazine/vault/A2596.cfm]

Sabelli, N., and Dede, C. (2000). Integrating educational research and practice: Reconceptualizing the goals and process of research to improve educational practice. [http://www.virtual.gmu.edu/SS_research/cdpapers/integrating.htm]

Sarasin, L. C. (1999). *Learning style perspectives: Impact in the classroom.* Madison, WI: Atwood.

Sawyer, J., and O'Fallon, T. (2000). The online phenomena of transformative learning. [http://leahi.kcc.hawaii.edu/tcon2k/paper/paper_sawyerj.html]

Schifter, C. C. (2000). Factors influencing faculty participation in distance education: A factor analysis. *ED at a Distance, 13*(1). [http://www.usdla.org/html/journal/JAN00_Issue/Factors.htm]

Schifter, C. (2002). Perception differences about participating in distance education. *Online Journal of Distance Learning Administration, 5*(1). [http://www.westga.edu/~distance/ojdla/spring51/schifter51.html]

Schommer, M., Crouse, A., and Rhodes, N. (1992). Epistemological beliefs and mathematical text comprehension: Believing it is simple does not make it so. *Journal of Educational Psychology, 82*(4), 435–443.

Schulman, A. H., and Sims, R. L. (1999). Learning in an online format versus an in-class format: An experimental study. *T.H.E. Journal, 26*(11). [http://www.thejournal.com/magazine/vault/A2090.cfm]

Schutte, J. G. (1997). Virtual teaching in higher education. [http://www.csun.edu/sociology/virexp.htm]

Schweiger, H. (1996). Quality in distance education and open learning. Minneapolis: Minnesota Higher Education Services Office. [http://www.heso.state.mn.us/www/reports/reports.htm]

Sener, J. (2001). Bring ALN into the mainstream: NVCC case studies II. *Online Education, 2,* 7–29.

Sener, J., and Stover, M. L. (2000). Integrating ALN into an independent study distance education program: NVCC case studies. *Journal of Asynchronous Learning Networks, 4*(2). [http://www.aln.org/alnweb/journal/Vol4_issue2/le/sener/le-sener.htm]

Serban, A. M. (2000). Evaluation of fall 1999 online courses. *ED at a Distance, 14*(10). [http://www.usdla.org/html/journal/OCT00_Issue/story04.htm]

Shapley, P. (2000). On-line education to develop complex reasoning skills in organic chemistry. *Journal of Asynchronous Learning Networks, 4*(2). [http://www.aln.org/alnweb/journal/Vol4_issue2/le/shapley/LE-shapley.htm]

Shaw, G. P., and Pieter, W. (2000). The use of asynchronous learning networks in nutrition education: Student attitude, experiences and performance. *Journal of Asynchronous Learning Networks, 4*(1). [http://www.aln.org/alnweb/journal/Vol4_issue1/shawpieter.htm]

Shea, P., and others. (2001). Measures of learning effectiveness in the SUNY learning network. *Online Education, 2,* 31–54.

Shell, B. (1994a). Shaping cyberspace into human space. [http//css.sfu.ca/update/vol6/6.3-harasim.main.html]

Shell, B. (1994b). Tips on shaping a virtual learning space.
[http://css.sfu.ca/update/vol6/6.3-tips-Virtual-Learning.html]

Shell, B. (1994c). Trouble in paradise.
[http://css.sfu.ca/update/vol6/6.3-trouble-in-paradise.html]

Short, N. M. (2000). Asynchronous distance education. *T.H.E. Journal, 28*(2).
[http://www.thejournal.com/magazine/vault/A3001.cfm]

Simonson, M., Smaldino, S., Albright, M., and Zvacek, S. (2000). *Teaching and learning at a distance*. Upper Saddle River, NJ: Prentice Hall.

Slay, J. (1999). The use of the Internet in creating an effective learning environment.
[http://ausweb.scu.edu.au/aw99_archive/aw99/proceedings/slay/paper.html]

Smith, G. G., Ferguson, D., and Caris, M. (2001). Teaching college courses online vs. face-to-face. *T.H.E. Journal, 28*(9).
[http://www.thejournal.com/magazine/vault/A3407.cfm]

Smith, P. L., and Dillon, C. (1999). Comparing distance learning and classroom learning: Conceptual considerations. *American Journal of Distance Education, 13*(2), 6–23.

Smith, S., Tyler, J. M., and Benscote, A. (2000). Internet supported teaching: Advice from the trenches. *ED at a Distance, 13*(1).
[http://www.usdla.org/html/journal/JAN00_Issue/Internet.htm]

Stinson, B. M., and Claus, K. (2000). The effects of electronic classrooms on learning English composition: A middle ground. *T.H.E. Journal, 27*(7).
[http://www.thejournal.com/magazine/vault/A2656.cfm]

Stith, B. (2000). Web-enhanced lecture course scores big with students and faculty. *T.H.E. Journal, 27*(8). [http://www.thejournal.com/magazine/vault/A2689.cfm]

Stone, T. E. (1992). A new look at the role of locus of control in completion rates in distance education. *Research in Distance Education, 4*(2), 6–9.

Stone, W. S., Showalter, E. D., Orig, A., and Grover, M. (2001). An empirical study of course selection and divisional structure in distance education programs. *Online Journal of Distance Learning Administration, 4*(1).
[http://www.westga.edu/~distance/ojdla/spring41/stone41.html]

Strong, R. W., and Harmon, E. G. (1997). Online graduate degrees: A review of three Internet-based master's degree offerings. *American Journal of Distance Education, 11*(3), 121–130.

Sulla, N. (1999, February). Technology: To use or infuse. *Technology Source.*
[http://horizon.unc.edu/TS/default.asp?show=article&id=46]

Sullivan, P. (1998). Gender issues and the on-line classroom.
[http://leahi.kcc.hawaii.edu/org/tcon98/paper/sullivan.html]

Tait, A. (1993). Systems, values and dissent: Quality assurance for open and distance learning. *Distance Education, 14*(2), 303–314.

Tait, A., and Mills, R. (eds.) (1999). *The convergence of distance and conventional education: Patterns of flexibility for the individual learner.* London: Routledge/ Falmer Press.

Talbott, S. (1995). The future does not compute. Sebastopol, CA: O'Reilly & Associates.

Talbott, S. (1999). Who's killing higher education? *Educom Review, 34*(2). [http://www.educause.edu/ir/library/html/erm99024.html]

Taylor, J. C. (1994). Technology, distance education and the tyranny of proximity. *Higher Education Management, 6*(2), 179–190.

Terry, N. (2001). Assessing enrollment and attrition rates for the online MBA. *T.H.E. Journal, 28*(7). [http://www.thejournal.com/magazine/vault/A3299.cfm]

Trentin, G. (2000). The quality-interactivity relationship in distance education. *Educational Technology, 40*(1), 17–27.

Tucker, S. (2001). Distance education: Better, worse, or as good as traditional education? *Online Journal of Distance Learning Administration, 4*(4). [http://www.westga.edu/~distance/ojdla/winter44/tucker44.html]

Tuckey, C. J. (1993). Computer conferencing and the electronic white board in the United Kingdom: A comparative analysis. *American Journal of Distance Education, 7*(2), 58–72.

Tuller, C., and Oblinger, D. (1999). Information technology as a transformation agent. [http://www.educause.edu/ir/library/html/cem9746.html]

Tulloch, J. B., and Sneed, J. R. (2000). Quality enhancing practices in distance education: Teaching and learning. Washington, DC: Instructional Telecommunications Council.

Turkle, S. (1995). *Life on the screen: Identity in the age of the Internet.* New York: Simon & Schuster.

Twigg, C. A. (1999, September 1). Who's teaching those online courses? The Learning MarketSpace. Listserv communication. [http://www.center.rpi.edu/Lforum/LdfLM.html]

Twigg, C. A. (2001a). Innovations in online learning. Pew Learning and Technology Program. Troy, NY: Center for Academic Transformation. [http://www.center.rpi.edu]

Twigg, C. A. (2001b). Quality assurance for whom? Providers and consumers in today's distributed learning environment. [http://www.center.rpi.edu/PewSym/mono3.html]

Twigg, C. A., and Heterick, R. C. (1997). The NLII vision: Implications for systems and states. [http://www.educom.edu/program/nlii/keydocs/publicpolicy.html]

U.S. Department of Education. (2000). Learning without limits: An agenda for the Office of Postsecondary Education. Washington, DC: U.S. Department of Education. [http://www.ed.gov/offices/OPE/AgenProj/report/index.html]

U.S. Department of Labor. (2001). Futurework. [http://www.dol.gov]

University of California-Los Angeles. (2001). Surveying the digital future: Year two. Los Angeles: Center for Communication Policy, University of California-Los Angeles.

Van Dusen, G. C. (2000). *Digital dilemma: Issues of access, cost, and quality in media-enhanced and distance education.* ASHE-ERIC Higher Education Report, vol. 27, no. 5. San Francisco: Jossey-Bass.

Visser, J. A. (2000). Faculty work in developing and teaching web-based distance courses: A case study of time and effort. *American Journal of Distance Education, 14*(3), 21–32.

Vrasidas, C., and McIsaac, M. S. (1999). Factors influencing interaction in an online course. *American Journal of Distance Education, 13*(3), 22–36.

Wade, W. (1999). What do students know and how do we know that they know it? *T.H.E. Journal, 27*(3). [http://www.thejournal.com/magazine/vault/A2291.cfm]

Web-Based Commission. (2001). The power of the Internet for learning: Moving from promise to practice. [http://www.ed.gov/offices/AC/WBEC/FinalReport/WBECReport.pdf]

Wegerif, R. (1998). The social dimension of asynchronous learning networks. *Journal of Asynchronous Learning Networks, 2*(1). [http://www.aln.org/alnweb/journal/Vol2_issue1/wegerif.htm]

Wegner, S. B., Holloway, K. C., and Garton, E. M. (1999). The effects of Internet-based instruction on student learning. *Journal of Asynchronous Learning Networks, 3*(2). [http://www.aln.org/alnweb/journal/Vol3_issue2/Wegner.htm]

Western Cooperative for Educational Telecommunications. (1995). Principles of good practice for electronically offered academic degree and certificate programs. [http://www.wiche.edu/telecom/projects/balancing/principles.htm]

Western Cooperative for Educational Telecommunications. (1995). *The distance learner's guide.* Upper Saddle River, NJ: Prentice Hall.

White, C. (2000). Students and faculty respond to online distance courses at Grant MacEwan Community College. *T.H.E. Journal, 27*(9). [http://www.thejournal.com/magazine/vault/A2814.cfm]

Whitesel, C. (1998, April). Reframing our classrooms, reframing ourselves: Perspectives from a virtual Paladin. *Technology Source.* [http://horizon.unc.edu/TS/default.asp?show=article&id=474]

Wideman, H., and Owston, R. D. (1999). Internet-based courses at Atkinson College: An initial assessment. [http://www.edu.yorku.ca/irlt/reports/techreport99-1.htm]

Wild, M., and Omari, A. (1996). A working model for designing learning environments. [http://www.scu.edu.au/sponsored/ausweb/ausweb96/educn/wild/paper.html]

Wilson, B. G. (1997). The postmodern paradigm. [http://carbon.cudenver.edu/~bwilson/postmodern.html]

Wilson, B., and Ryder, M. (2001). Dynamic learning communities: An alternative to designed instructional systems. [http://carbon.cudenver.edu/~mryder/dlc.html]

Wisher, R. A., and Curnow, C. K. (1999). Perceptions and effects of image transmissions during Internet-based training. *American Journal of Distance Education, 13*(3), 37–51.

Wolcott, L. L. (1997). Tenure, promotion, and distance education: Examining the culture of faculty rewards. *American Journal of Distance Education, 11*(2), 3–18.

Wolf, D. B., and Johnstone, S. M. (1999). Cleaning up the language. *Change, 31*(4), 34–40.

Young, J. R. (2002, March 22). "Hybrid" teaching seeks to end the divide between traditional and online instruction. *Chronicle of Higher Education, 48*(28), A33. [http://chronicle.com/free/v48/i28/28a03301.htm]

Name Index

A

Abernathy, D. J., 86
Abrami, P. C., 43
Alley, L. R., 85, 93
Altnay, A., 51
Amundsen, C., 43
Anderson, T., 47, 59
Arbaugh, D. J., 59
Archer, W., 47, 59
Arvan, L., 61

B

Barker, K., 80
Barr, R. B., 25
Baxter, J. T., 63
Baylen, D. M., 45
Becker, D., 49
Bellcourt, M. A., 50
Benbunan-Fich, R., 31
Bendixen, L. D., 43
Benscote, A., 56
Berge, Z. L., 17, 64, 66, 67
Berns, R. G., 25
Bernt, F. L., 42
Betts, K. S., 57
Biner, P. M., 42
Bink, M. L., 42
Bleck, B., 26
Blum, K. D., 46
Boaz, M., 84
Boettcher, J. V., 85
Bontenbal, K. F., 49
Bothun, G. D., 44

Bourne, J. R., 14
Boyer, E. L., 99, 102
Brooks, D., 43
Brown, B., 25, 32
Brown, G., 17, 18, 19, 35, 74, 103
Brown, J. S., 25, 71
Brown, R., 38
Buchanan, E. A., 64
Bugbee, A. C., 42
Bullock, C., 45
Burbules, N. C., 25, 30
Bures, E. M., 43
Burnaska, K., 45
Burton, J. K., 16

C

Callister, T. A., 25, 30
Campbell, J. O., 14
Campos, M., 31, 36
Carabajal, K., 92
Cárdenas, K., 57
Caris, M., 61, 64, 67
Carr, S., 86
Cavanaugh, S., 58
Cennamo, K. S., 43
Cerny, M. G., 43
Chickering, A. W., 41, 78, 83
Clark, R. E., 14, 16, 41, 65
Claus, K., 45
Cochrane, C., 47
Conrad, R., 85
Coppola, N. W., 36, 59
Corderoy, R. M., 84

Ory, J. C., 45
Osborne, V., 45
Owston, R. D., 14

P

Palattella, J., 6
Palloff, R. M., 36, 37, 38
Parker, D., 31
Pascarella, E. T., 33
Paskey, J., 31
Perrin, D. G., 69
Phipps, R. A., 16, 17, 80
Pierson, C. T., 33
Pieter, W., 44
Pimentel, J. R., 25
Pratt, K., 36, 37, 38
Presby, L., 61
Privateer, P. M., 72

R

Ragan, L. C., 78
Reeves, B., 41
Rhodes, N., 43
Ridley, D., 14
Rieger, J., 14
Roblyer, M. D., 34
Rockwell, S. K., 58
Roger, E. M., 62
Rogers, C. S., 43
Ross, J. D., 43
Rotter N., 59
Rourke, L., 59
Russell, T. L., 13, 14, 16, 30, 31
Rutherford, P., 32
Ryan, R. C., 14
Ryder, M., 37

S

Sarasin, L. C., 48
Sawyer, J., 26
Schauer, J., 58
Schifter, C. C., 56
Schnecbeck, C. A., 62
Schommer, M., 43
Schulman, A. H., 14
Schutte, J. G., 31

Schweiger, H., 9, 81
Sener, J., 14, 33
Serban, A. M., 14
Shapley, P., 47
Shaw, G. P., 44
Shell, B., 35, 37, 84
Shepherd, M., 14
Shoemaker, J., 32
Short, N. M., 84
Showalter, E. D., 68
Sims, R. L., 14
Slay, J., 39
Smith, G. G., 60, 64, 67
Smith, P. L., 65
Smith, S., 56
Sneed, J. R., 78
Sokenu, J., 61
Spiro, R. J., 43, 46
Stinson, B. M., 45
Stith, B., 59
Stone, T. E., 48
Stone, W. S., 68
Stover, M. L., 14
Strong, R. W., 86
Sulla, N., 58
Sullivan, P., 46

T

Tabata, L., 37
Tagg, J., 25
Tait, A., 68, 80, 99
Talbott, S., 40, 71
Taylor, J. C., 68
Terry, N., 43
Thompson, M. M., 17
Trentin, G., 34
Trotter, N., 36
Truman-Davis, B., 61
Tucker, S., 32
Tuckey, C. J., 30
Tuller, C., 53, 73
Tulloch, J. B., 78
Turkle, S., 40
Turoff, M., 31, 36
Twigg, C. A., 50, 73, 96, 97
Tyler, J. M., 45, 56

V

Van Dusen, G. C., 72
Vesper, N., 33, 48
Visser, J. A., 61
Vrasidas, C., 34

W

Wack, M., 17, 18, 19, 35
Wade, W., 48, 70
Webb, B., 47
Wegerif, R., 35, 48
Wegner, S. B., 14
Weller, M., 44
Wellman, J. V., 80
Wheatley, M., 74
White, C., 59

Whitesel, C., 48
Wideman, H., 14
Wild, M., 34
Wilger, A. K., 99
Wilson, B., 37
Wilson, B. G., 27
Wisher, R. A., 63
Wolcott, L. L., 58
Wolf, D. B., 69

Y

Young, J. R., 31

Z

Zittle, F. J., 59

Subject Index

A

AAUP (American Association of University Professors), 10

"Academic self-concept," 42–43

Accreditation:
associations governing, 8–9
latest thinking on distance education, 82–83

AFT (American Federation of Teachers), 10, 16, 81–82

Agenda Project (U.S. Department of Education), 5

ALNs (asynchronous learning networks) studies
on building learning communities, 38–39
on faculty satisfaction with, 60–61
on impact of ALN on improved writing skills, 48
on "pedagogical-action clusters," 36*fig*
on social element of ALNs, 35
on student attitude, motivation, preparation, 44
on student success rates/satisfaction, 33
on withdrawal rates/success rates, 32
See also Distance education

American Center for the Study of Distance Education, 17, 21

American Chemical Society exam, 47

American Council on Education, 79

American Federation of Teachers, 73

AQIP (Academic Quality Improvement Project), 94–95

B

Barron's Guide to Distance Learning, 86

Bear's Guide to Earning Degrees Nontraditionally, 86

Behaviorism theory, 24

Best Distance Learning Graduate Programs (Princeton Review), 86

British Open University, 6

C

The Campus Computing Project survey, 3–4

CHEA (Council for Higher Education Accreditation), 79, 80, 81, 83, 84*t*

Cheyney University, 77

Cognitive flexibility theory, 47

Cognitive presence, 47

Cognitive theory, 27–28

Collaboration:
on-line learning communities and, 35–39
"Pedagogical-action clusters" model of, 36*fig*
technological support of learning, 34–35

Commodification of higher education, 7

Competency standards, 81

Conceptual model of education, 71–72

Constructed identity concept, 40

Constructivism theory, 24–27

Contextual learning, 25

Council for Higher Education Accreditation, 9

ASHE-ERIC
Higher Education Reports

The mission of the Educational Resources Information Center (ERIC) system is to improve American education by increasing and facilitating the use of educational research and information on practice in the activities of learning, teaching, educational decision making, and research, wherever and whenever these activities take place.

Since 1983, the ASHE-ERIC Higher Education Report series has been published in cooperation with the Association for the Study of Higher Education (ASHE). Starting in 2000, the series has been published by Jossey-Bass in conjunction with the ERIC Clearinghouse on Higher Education.

Each monograph is the definitive analysis of a tough higher education problem, based on thorough research of pertinent literature and institutional experiences. Topics are identified by a national survey. Noted practitioners and scholars are then commissioned to write the reports, with experts providing critical reviews of each manuscript before publication.

Six monographs in the series are published each year and are available on individual and subscription bases. To order, use the order form at the back of this issue.

Qualified persons interested in writing a monograph for the series are invited to submit a proposal to the National Advisory Board. As the preeminent literature review and issue analysis series in higher education, the Higher Education Reports are guaranteed wide dissemination and provide national exposure for accepted candidates. Execution of a monograph requires at least a minimal familiarity with the ERIC database, including *Resources in Education* and the current *Index to Journals in Education*. The objective of these reports is to bridge conventional wisdom and practical research.

Advisory Board

Susan Frost
Office of Institutional Planning
and Research
Emory University

Kenneth Feldman
SUNY at Stony Brook

Anna Ortiz
Michigan State University

James Fairweather
Michigan State University

Lori White
Stanford University

Esther E. Gottlieb
West Virginia University

Carol Colbeck
Pennsylvania State University

Jeni Hart
University of Arizona

Review Panelists and Consulting Editors

Robert J. Barak
Board of Regents, State of Iowa

Jeffrey A. Cantor
Norwalk Community College

Michael D. Corry
The George Washington
University

Jennifer Hart
Center for the Study of Higher
Education, University of Arizona

Donald E. Heller
Pennsylvania State University

Edward R. Hines
Illinois State University

Russ Poulin
Western Cooperative for
Educational Telecommunications

Recent Titles

Back Issue/Subscription Order Form

Copy or detach and send to:

Jossey-Bass, A Wiley Company, 989 Market Street, San Francisco CA 94103-1741

Call or fax toll-free: Phone 888-378-2537 6:30AM – 3PM PST; Fax 888-481-2665

Back Issues: Please send me the following issues at $24 each
(Important: please include series abbreviation and issue number.
For example AEHE28:1)

_____

_____

_____

$ _____ Total for single issues

$ _____ SHIPPING CHARGES: SURFACE   Domestic Canadian
                                    First Item $5.00 $6.00
                                    Each Add'l Item $3.00 $1.50
                    For next-day and second-day delivery rates, call the number listed above.

Subscriptions Please ❑ start ❑ renew my subscription to *ASHE-ERIC Higher Education Reports* for the year 2_____at the following rate:

U.S.	❑ Individual $150	❑ Institutional $150
Canada	❑ Individual $150	❑ Institutional $230
All Others	❑ Individual $198	❑ Institutional $261
Online Subscription		❑ Institutional $150

**For more information about online subscriptions visit
www.interscience.wiley.com**

$ _____ Total single issues and subscriptions (Add appropriate sales tax for your state for single issue orders. No sales tax for U.S. subscriptions. Canadian residents, add GST for subscriptions and single issues.)

❑Payment enclosed (U.S. check or money order only)
❑VISA ❑ MC ❑ AmEx ❑ Discover Card #_____ Exp. Date _____

Signature _____ Day Phone _____
❑ Bill Me (U.S. institutional orders only. Purchase order required.)

Purchase order # _____
　　　　　　　　Federal Tax ID13559302　　　　　　**GST 89102 8052**

Name _____

Address _____

_____

Phone _____ E-mail _____

For more information about Jossey-Bass, visit our Web site at www.josseybass.com

PROMOTION CODE ND03

ASHE-ERIC HIGHER EDUCATION REPORT
IS NOW AVAILABLE ONLINE AT WILEY INTERSCIENCE

What is Wiley InterScience?

Wiley InterScience is the dynamic online content service from John Wiley &
Sons delivering the full text of over 300 leading scientific, technical, medical,
and professional journals, plus major reference works, the acclaimed Current
Protocols laboratory manuals, and even the full text of select Wiley print books
online.

What are some special features of Wiley InterScience?

Wiley Interscience Alerts is a service that delivers table of contents via e-mail
for any journal available on Wiley InterScience as soon as a new issue is
published online.
Early View is Wiley's exclusive service presenting individual articles online as
soon as they are ready, even before the release of the compiled print issue.
These articles are complete, peer-reviewed, and citable.
CrossRef is the innovative multi-publisher reference linking system enabling
readers to move seamlessly from a reference in a journal article to the cited
publication, typically located on a different server and published by a different
publisher.

How can I access Wiley InterScience?

Visit http://www.interscience.wiley.com.

Guest Users can browse Wiley InterScience for unrestricted access to journal
Tables of Contents and Article Abstracts, or use the powerful search engine.
Registered Users are provided with a *Personal Home Page* to store and
manage customized alerts, searches, and links to favorite journals and articles.
Additionally, Registered Users can view free Online Sample Issues and preview
selected material from major reference works.
Licensed Customers are entitled to access full-text journal articles in PDF, with
select journals also offering full-text HTML.

How do I become an Authorized User?

Authorized Users are individuals authorized by a paying Customer to have
access to the journals in Wiley InterScience. For example, a University that
subscribes to Wiley journals is considered to be the Customer.
Faculty, staff and students authorized by the University to have access to those
journals in Wiley InterScience are Authorized Users. Users should contact their
Library for information on which Wiley journals they have access to in
Wiley InterScience.

ASK YOUR INSTITUTION ABOUT WILEY INTERSCIENCE TODAY!

Katrina A. Meyer is currently an assistant professor of educational leadership at the University of North Dakota, with a special interest in Web-based learning and distance education in higher education institutions. For more than three years, she was director of distance learning and technology at the University and Community College System of Nevada, where she helped create a systemwide Web-based catalogue for all distance education courses. From 1988 to 1998, she was associate director of academic affairs at the Higher Education Coordinating Board for the State of Washington, where she was responsible for policy and planning for technology and distance education issues.